Tattooed Without a Choice

Tattooed Without a Choice

John Karsay

Copyright © 2005 John Karsay
All rights reserved.

ISBN : 1-4196-2098-3

To order additional copies, please contact us.
BookSurge, LLC
www.booksurge.com
1-866-308-6235
orders@booksurge.com

Tattooed Without a Choice

We see them in the streets digging through our garbage cans. We see them in the subways begging for our change. We see them living on park benches panhandling, then nodding off from the drugs they are on. Across the United States, we see them incarcerated in our prisons. Though we never take the time to find out what altered their lives, we'll judge them and develop our own conclusions about them. Surely it wasn't decided in the early stages of their lives, or when they were born, that they were going to be homeless, drug addicts, or criminals. How many of us asked the question, "Why doesn't he get a job?" How many of us ever wondered, "How could somebody live like that?" Or, "What would make him do that?" It is unfortunate that the answers to these questions are rarely answered correctly. We live in a society in which we marginalize and label people. As long as this common practice continues, the cycle of homelessness, crime, and addiction will as well. If one judges people by their actions and labels them, without knowing the cause, he will not be able to prevent such actions from occurring and reoccurring. The life of convicted murderer Anthony Pagano convinces me I am right.

Pagano's background having a lot of similarities to my own—his age, his Italian descent, the fact that he was from the same neighborhood in Brooklyn—he did not strike me as a hardened criminal. I wanted to discover why a person so much like myself would need to commit such a desperate act as murder. My first impression of Anthony was that he was a spoiled brat from the neighborhood who decided to avoid work and make money unethically. The middle—to upper-class Italian neighborhood we grew up in consisted of many kids who did not have a lot of pressure on them to work—or to do anything, for that matter. Most of the time these kids could be seen hanging around the streets or driving around in Cadillacs purchased by their parents. Just about every household in the neighborhood consisted of the same cast of characters: the father, who either owned his own business or held some form of good paying Union job; the mother, who stayed home and took care of the house and the children; and the children—at least two of them, since an Italian family would not be complete without at least one girl and one boy.

As Anthony told his story, my perception of him changed. Although he was in the third year of his sentence and quite eager to discuss the turn of events that led him to his present situation, his tone of voice was still uncomfortable when he spoke about his last day of freedom. Almost (but not quite) with a stutter, Anthony described the day and his state of mind. There was a shame in his eyes, which could best be described as the shame of a married man of twenty years who had just been caught in the act of adultery. Anthony attempted to clear his crackling, remorseful voice. I thought: This man barely knows me. In an effort to calm him down, I asked, "Are you alright?"

Not trying to avoid looking me in the eyes, yet keeping his head halfway down, Anthony replied, "Yeah, I'm fine."

Being polite, and at the same time attempting to cheer him up a bit, I asked, "Could I get you something? Water? Soda? Coffee?" Jokingly I added, "A beer?"

With a smile and a more relaxed look on his face, Anthony said, "No thanks. Maybe later." More comfortable now, Anthony added, "It is really funny you mentioned beer."

Wondering if Anthony thought I was serious about the beer, and a little curious, I inquired, "Oh yeah, why is that?" Glad to answer, Anthony replied, "Well, because beer, alcohol, and of course other things were just the beginning of all my problems." Wanting Anthony to elaborate, and assuring him he was not alone, I replied, "You know something? It is for a lot of people." Anthony was about to respond when I quickly interrupted. "Wait, I have an idea."

Now exited, Anthony said, "Oh yeah, what's that?"

Quickly explaining, I responded, "Since you mentioned beer and alcohol being the root of all your problems, instead of talking about that day of the incident, why don't we talk about that? Let us find out how you ended up getting to the day of your arrest."

With a look of relief on his face, Anthony said, "Where should I start?"

"Why don't you begin with your family?"

Anthony was born in the early 1970s, the fourth and last child in a very unstable marriage. Anthony's parents, Joseph Pagano and Angela Manfreddi, were both third-generation immigrants and who married during the hippie days of the late 1960s. Although both came from traditional religious backgrounds, their family values had somehow been lost during the times. Their first child—Anthony's oldest sister, Catholina—was named after Angela's mother. After her birth, Joseph and Angela vowed to give up their wild ways and become responsible parents. Joseph's appliance repair shop began to do very well, and one year later he and Angela tried to complete their family with a son. But to Joseph's disappointment, as fate would have it, the couple's next child was a girl too. Distraught by this outcome, and determined to have a namesake, Joseph decided to name their second daughter Josephina. A couple of years later, the business still doing well, Joseph and Angela once again attempted to have the son they were both longing for. This time they were successful, though unfortunately by this time a new problem had emerged. Joseph, using the excuse that he was unable to father a son, broke his vow of sobriety and fell off the wagon. Before long, Joseph's drinking had become both excessive and destructive. Maybe to some people drinking abusively every day may not do much harm in their lives; for Joseph, however, drinking would prove to be his complete downfall. For the effects of alcohol are different for every individual. Alcohol can make people happy, or sad, or angry, or just plain tired. For some, alcohol can even be an aphrodisiac. But for Joseph, alcohol put him in a paranoid, almost psychotic,,state of mind.

After the birth of Anthony's older brother, Joseph Jr., Joseph convinced himself the boy did not belong to him. After all her sacrifices and loyalty, it would have been ludicrous to think that

Angela would ever commit adultery. But already in Joseph Sr.'s mind was the notion that it was impossible for him to conceive a boy, and it didn't help that Joseph Jr., who had been born with blonde hair and blue eyes, didn't resemble his father at all. Was Joseph Sr. really that delusional? Or was it what he needed to believe in order to have a reason to continue drinking? In any event, as Anthony put it, the use of alcohol would become the beginning of the problems yet to come for this family for years.

Still seeing a lot of good in her husband, Angela did not want to give up on her marriage. In hope of reforming Joseph into the man he had once been, Angela conceived the couple's fourth and final child, Anthony. Angela's devotion, though admirable, would prove to be in vain. At the time of Anthony's birth, Joseph Sr. was too far gone into alcoholism to save. By the time Anthony was two, Joseph had already lost his business and their house, and was up to his eyebrows in debt. It would not be long before what usually happens next. When an alcoholic is faced with all of these type of financial woes, that is when the three big A's come into play: aggravation, abuse, and abandonment. I found it very sad to hear Anthony's memories of the beatings. I couldn't imagine having my first childhood trauma being inflicted by the hands of my father.

How can a boy overcome this kind of betrayal? How does one ever get over it when his first memory of his father is the back of his hand and the last is the police dragging him out of his life forever?

It was of course obvious that Angela had no choice but to get her family out of that situation. Angela knew that eventually one of Joseph's drunken episodes would escalate into something fatal for her or the kids. Although Angela was a strong woman and was willing to do the best for her family, it doesn't take a genius to realize the road ahead would be a rough one for her. Even in today's world, with all the resources available to single parents, only a miracle from above could allow someone to raise four small children by themselves without something being compromised. Now just imagine how difficult it would have been for a single parent during the 1970s.

Being left penniless and with no food whatsoever by Joseph Sr., Anthony remembers eating only crackers and cheese for the first couple of days after his father's departure. Relying on her family a little just to eat, Angela then began looking for work to support her family. With limited skills, and her children being too young to take care of themselves, it was impossible for her to find any work. She had no choice but to go on welfare. But it wasn't as easy as it sounded. The welfare system is not quick to help if you are not a minority. Angela was required to provide written documentation that she had no family members able to help her support her and her family. It took weeks of near-starvation before welfare disbursed anything.

I suppose the transition from middle-class to poverty would have been more difficult for Angela if it had happened suddenly. But since Joseph Sr. had already started the process for her, Angela had a taste of poverty already. The children, however, had a more difficult time adjusting. Not able to understand the challenges their mother was facing, they became bitter over the lack of luxuries in their lives. Imagine seeing your friends getting all the extra perks, and you are not able to enjoy the same, not even something as simple as an ice cream cone. Imagine having to eat fish sticks while you watch your friends enjoying barbecues. Most children who grow up with feelings of envy, anger, and sadness usually react in one of two ways. Either they take their frustration out on somebody else, or they keep it bottled up inside of them. Keep in mind that years ago, unlike today, children did not disrespect their parents in any way. It can be very much assumed that concealing rage would become common for Angela's children.

Being materially deprived is not the only disadvantage of coming from a broken home. When only one parent is available for four children, the amount of attention she can provide is scarce and often inadequate. The majority of the time, the children were inadequately supervised. Boys in particular are generally attracted to mischief. Easily influenced, often at the hands of his older brother, Anthony would be coerced into doing things that would have displeased Angela.

Even though in the 1970s parents were able to discipline their children much more severely than today, that didn't stop Angela's boys from getting into trouble. In most cases, out of fear of his older brother, Anthony would have to do the actual misdeed. The first example of this was in public school. Although Joseph Jr. was two years older than Anthony, they shared the same school library. Because many were not returned, the school had a strict rule that no books were to be removed from school premises. Not so much Anthony, but Joseph Jr.'s interest in reading was above average. However, Joseph Jr. often had trouble finishing books because of the school's policy. One book in particular Joseph Jr. wanted more than any other. Knowing how gullible his little brother was, and not wanting to risk getting caught himself, Joseph Jr. managed to intimidate Anthony into stealing the book for him. By simply putting it in his bag with his other books, then walking out, Anthony didn't have any trouble getting the book out of the library. However, another dilemma did exist. Anthony was only in the first grade and really did not know how to read yet. Without much help from his older brother, it took Anthony twenty attempts before finally taking the book Joseph Jr. actually wanted.

Not too long after this, while cleaning the boy's room, Angela discovered all the extra books piling up. Knowing that she had not bought the books for them, Angela called the boys in from outside to confront them. The first one in from outside was Joseph Jr. Because only he was able to read, Angela figured the books belonged to him. After denying he knew where the books came from, Joseph Jr. was severely beaten until he told his mother the truth. Afterward, Angela called Anthony inside. In a loud and scary voice she asked, "Anthony! Did you steal these books from school?"

Seeing his brother in pain, and as any scared child would, Anthony said, " No." Already furious because of what the boys did, Angela slapped Anthony across the face and said, "Anthony, don't lie to me!" Staring her youngest boy in the face with a look as if she were about to strike again, she asked, "Anthony, did you steal these books for your brother from school?"

At the moment Anthony realized that Joseph Jr. had cracked and that his mother knew everything anyway. Backing away in an attempt to avoid getting hit again, Anthony answered, "Yeah."

After a slight moment—just enough time for Anthony to get his guard down—Angela grabbed him around the waist from an overhead position. With his arms and his head between her left hip and her left arm, Angela began vigorously and repeatedly spanking Anthony on his buttocks with her right hand. Between each strike to her son's bottom, Angela yelled over and over, "This is what you get for stealing. This is what you get for lying."

Angela was a frustrated single parent and had built up a lot of anger and rage towards her ex-husband. When she became upset, she would direct all that anger towards her children.

But it was very easy for Joseph Jr. to talk Anthony into doing anything. And so Anthony would face many beatings at the hands of his mother for years to come. However, Anthony did have an alternative. He could refuse the orders demanded by his older brother and then take the beating handed down by him. But in truth, Anthony could not win. The only chance Anthony had was not to get caught doing whatever it was he shouldn't be doing. Thus could Anthony avoid the beating from Joseph Jr. and any disciplinary action from Angela. To an unknowing eye, it may have seemed that Anthony was abused. The beatings Anthony had to endure may even appear cruel and horrific at times. In the long run, though, Anthony would become much tougher than other kids his age. Anthony's tolerance to pain increased to a point where he even became immune to it.

Although Anthony's toughness and ability to fight were now strong, he still would not be able to win in a fight against his bullish older brother. It wasn't that Joseph Jr. was a better fighter than Anthony; it wasn't that Joseph Jr. was any stronger than Anthony. In truth, because of his slim yet muscular build, Anthony was even stronger than his older brother. Indeed Joseph Jr. was taller and heavier than Anthony, but Anthony had more speed. The only reason Anthony could not win fights was simply psychological. Because of the intimidation factor, older brothers in general always have an upper edge over their younger brothers. The confidence level of the older brother will always give him that extra control. When the fights did occur between the two, it was very rare that Anthony ever struck back at Joseph Jr. Anthony would just lie back and take the beating—during which, he would try to block as many punches as possible. These fights usually ended when Joseph Jr. either got tired or finished letting out whatever rage was inside of him. In any event, you have to give credit to where credit is due. Contrary to what most people think, Anthony's unwillingness to fight his older brother was not a sign of weakness; many would even consider it respectful. Nothing could be further from the truth than to consider Anthony weak. Anthony's ability to endure pain would be displayed throughout the remainder of his life.

Anthony's toughness would first be demonstrated at the tender age of six. One day, Anthony had plunged to the ground from the second floor of the house in which his family was living at the time. The house itself consisted of two stories and was the middle house in a block in which all the houses were attached and identical. Converted into three apartments by the owner, the house itself was originally built for one family. There was the basement apartment; ideal for a single person or a college student, it consisted of one bedroom, a living room, a bathroom and a kitchen. Dominic, the occupant of the basement apartment at the time, was a single man in his twenties who worked as a plumber. A quiet man, Dominic kept to himself and rarely let his presence be known. The second apartment, located on the ground floor of the house, was set up much like the basement apartment. The difference between the basement apartment and the ground-floor apartment was the two extra bedrooms. Also, whoever occupied the ground-floor apartment had full use of the back yard. After the departure of Joseph Sr., the Paganos had to vacate the ground-floor apartment for the less expensive second-floor apartment. At this time, Steve and Joan O'Hera, a young Irish couple, moved in with their only daughter, Tammy. At the time the Paganos occupied the ground floor apartment,

TATTOOED WITHOUT A CHOICE

Joseph Sr. made it quite adequate and luxurious for the[m], a swimming pool in the back yard surrounded by a vege[table] garden started by Angela. So it was quite a step down wh[en] Angela had to give up the apartment. Although the top-floor apartment had just as many rooms, they were less spacious. Without the use of the back yard for her four kids, Angela had to make many adjustments. Occupied by the kids, the boys in one and the girls in the other, the two bedrooms faced the front of the house. Separated by the hallway where the bathroom was located, the living room and the kitchen were adjacent to each other in the rear of the apartment. Without a bedroom for herself, Angela slept on a sofa bed in the living room. Covering the porch of the house, outside the window of the boy's room there was an overhead roof. Supported by two poles that led to the porch, the roof was shaped like a triangle.

The family's only television—a twelve-inch black-and-white set that had a coat hanger for an antenna and pliers on the side to change the channels—was located in the living room where Angela slept. Not allowed to watch television until Angela woke up, especially on weekends, the children would have to find something else to do in the meantime. Due to the lack of money, the children didn't have many toys to play with. Well, what about Christmas and their birthdays? you might ask. Didn't some of their relatives buy the children toys for these occasions? The answer to this is both yes and no. Yes, Angela's family did provide her children with gifts for their birthdays and Christmas. No, rarely did the children receive toys as presents. The reason was, Angela requested her children receive clothes instead. Unable to work because of the ages of her children, and welfare not providing sufficient money to clothe four children, Angela had little choice but to make this request. So with only their imaginations to work with, finding something else to do while they waited for their mother to wake up wasn't that easy. To many, this may not seem bad or harmful in any way. For girls, who in general are more mature and have a much calmer demeanor than boys, it is true. Matter of fact, for girls, having an active imagination is quite healthy. However, for boys, ng an active imagination can be downright dangerous. The difference is that girls will draw, read, play tea party, or invent other creative activities. Boys, on the other hand, tend to be more attracted to physical activities such as running around the house, jumping up and down on the bed, wrestling, or fighting. It was all these circumstances combined that led to the time Anthony plunged to the ground from two stories up.

One Saturday morning, while Angela was still asleep, Catholina and Josephina were in their room, playing house. Joseph Jr. decided that he and Anthony were going to play Batman and Robin. Batman and Robin was not based on the Batman and Robin movies, which have just came out recently. The boys were going to play Batman and Robin based on the television show from the 1960s. In the show, before going out to fight crime, the dynamic duo needed to slide down the poles, which turned them into Batman and Robin. In order to make the game more realistic, so they too could turn into Batman and Robin, Joseph Jr. and Anthony would have to find two poles to slide down. It wasn't good enough for Joseph Jr. to just imagine they were sliding down poles and turning into their favorite superheroes; the game wouldn't be complete unless they actually did it. In Joseph's eyes, only one part of the house would accommodate this desire. Not knowing for certain whether the roof of the porch, which was right outside their window, was strong enough to hold them, Joseph Jr. insisted Anthony try first. Of course, Anthony's answer to Joseph Jr.'s request was no. The answer coming from his little brother, whom he had so much control over, was unacceptable to Joseph Jr. At that point, it wasn't even about playing the game anymore. Anthony was going to go out on that roof simply because Joseph Jr. told him to. Very frightened to go out there, and attempting to get his older brother to change his mind, Anthony pleaded, "Joey, please, I'm scared. Please don't make me go out there."

Barking back in a stern yet low voice, Joseph Jr. said, "Shhh, be quiet, you're gonna wake mommy up." Then, wondering why Anthony didn't want to obey him, Joseph Jr. added, "Why not? Don't you want to be Robin?"

With the classic sad puppy dog face that all children have, Anthony answered, "I'm scared I'm gonna fall and die." Speaking softly, demandingly, and convincingly, Joseph Jr. replied, "You're not gonna fall. All you have to do is grab the pole and slide down to the porch." Concerned, Anthony asked, "What happens if I fall and die, though?" Becoming angry by his little brother's stalling, Joseph Jr. responded, "Don't be stupid, ya not gonna fall, and ya not gonna die." Then, clenching his fist and waving it in front of Anthony's face in order to make sure that he did not defy him, Joseph added, "I tell you what, if you don't go out there, you will die because I will kill you."

Without a choice, Anthony proceeded to climb out the window, honoring Joseph Jr.'s demand. The roof was wet and slippery—not from rain but from the morning mist. Anthony climbed out very cautiously. Once outside, he positioned his feet so that he would have one on each side of the triangular arch. With his older brother rooting him on, Anthony made his way toward the end of the roof. Even though it was only a few feet from the base of the boy's window to his destination, it felt like a lifetime before Anthony reached his goal. Finally reaching the end of the roof—with a look of despair on his face, a worried sound in his voice, searching for assistance from his older brother—Anthony asked, "Joey, what I do now?"

Attempting to coach Anthony, Joseph Jr. responded, ""Grab the pole and slide down." Trying to accomplish what Joseph Jr. wanted him to, a frustrated Anthony replied, "I can't. The pole is too far; I can't reach it."

Joseph Jr. didn't want to hear this. He was determined that it was possible to slide down the pole. Becoming extremely frightened, and with one last plea for his brother to give up this ludicrous idea, Anthony shouted, "I ain't doing this Joey, I'm comin' back in."

Feeling angry, disrespected, and nervous that their mother was going to wake up from all the commotion, Joseph Jr. rapidly closed the window—the only reentry Anthony had into the apartment. Simultaneously, Joseph Jr. began pointing in Anthony's direction and said, "The only way you get in is by going down." Then in a heartless manner, Joseph pulled the shade to the window and walked away.

Imagine being a six-year-old left in this type of situation. What would you do? Probably the exact same thing Anthony did at the moment. That's right, Anthony began to scream and cry. Because of the squatted position in which he'd been left—on all fours and holding on for dear life—it was not possible for Anthony to bang on or break the window to his room. Finally, after about ten minutes, the window to Anthony's sisters' room opened.

The first head to peak out was Josephina's. Turning pale, her mouth dropping wide open, she asked, "What the hell you doin' out there?"

A little relieved, yet still frightened, Anthony responded, "Joey locked me out."

Curious, Josephina asked, "Why?"

"Because he wants me to slide down the pole," Anthony answered. Then, with a dumbfounded look on her face, Josephina asked, "Do you need help?" Responding urgently, Anthony pleaded, "Yeah, please go open the window in my room." Honoring her baby brother's request, Josephina replied, "Okay, wait there." Josephina retreated from her window to attempt to let Anthony back in the apartment.

After about five minutes, Josephina returned. Sticking her head out of the window and attempting to get her brother's attention, she called out, "Anthony!"

Disappointed that his sister was back in her room and hadn't open the window, Anthony said, "What?"

After explaining what went wrong, Josephina informed her little brother, "Joey won't open the door to your room." Becoming desperate, Anthony asked in a very sad voice, "Why don't you get mommy?" Concerned for her own well-being, Josephina responded, "Because he said if I did he'll kick my ass too. He also said he is teaching you a lesson. What's that mean? What lesson?"

Beginning to cry, Anthony continued to plead to his sister, and requested, "Help me. I don't want to die."

Touched by Anthony's dilemma and realizing she needed to do something to help her baby brother, Josephina—in an effort to calm him—said, "Don't worry Anthony. I have an idea. I'll save you, but I got to go get something."

Josephina walked away then returned about a minute later with their mother's broom. She stuck the broom out of the window and instructed Anthony, "Grab this, and I'll pull you in."

Having many doubts, yet desperate, Anthony asked, "You think it will work? Are you strong enough? Why don't you get Catholina to help you?" Confidently Josephina replied, "Na, I can do it. Catholina is in the shower."

Willing to try anything at this point just to get off the roof, and grabbing hold of the other end of the broom, Anthony said, "Okay, but don't let me go, please."

Josephina nodded yes and then proceeded to hold the broom very tightly, as Anthony did on the other end. As luck would have it, at the exact moment Anthony was about to be pulled in, Catholina walked into her room. She startled Josephina by asking, "What are yous doin'?"

Without realizing what she had done, Josephina reacted to her sister by letting go of the broom. Then, in an instant, Josephina—quickly turning back around toward Anthony—gasped fearfully, rolled her eyes up to God, and folded her hands in a praying motion. Just about to cry, Josephina said aloud, "Oh my God, I'm so sorry." Realizing her mistake as she watched Anthony lose his balance and fall helplessly to the ground., Josephina turned to her older sister with a guilty look on her face. Beginning to cry, Josephina—in desperate need of guidance—asked Catholina, "What do I do?" Very concerned, Catholina replied, "Why? What happened?" Becoming hysterical, Josephina walked toward her older sister expecting a hug of comfort and said, "I just killed Anthony." Catholina reacted by rushing to the window. Instead of giving Josephina the hug she was excting, Catholina pushed her aside with one arm.

Catholina, always the most responsible of the children,

looked out of her window to check on Anthony. As Josephina continued to cry and explain what had happened, Catholina disregarded everything she was saying and called down to her little brother. "Anthony, are you okay?"

Clutching his left arm with his right, unable to speak from the shock of what had just happened, Anthony looked up toward Catholina and just shook his head no.

In an effort to try and console Anthony, Catholina—using a confident tone—called down to her little brother and said, "Don't worry Anthony, you're gonna be alright. I'm getting mommy."

Even in excruciating pain, Anthony did not cry until he heard what Catholina said. He wasn't worried that he may have been seriously injured, nor did he care that he'd almost died. Anthony's biggest fear was the reaction of his mother once she found out the mischief that he and his siblings were just involved in. Catholina, though, was thinking more rationally. Despite worrying herself what her mother's reaction would be, Catholina rushed to the living room to wake up Angela. Being the oldest, Catholina was in charge of the other children whenever their mother wasn't available for any reason. This meant that Catholina was responsible for anything the other children did as well. Even with this in mind, Catholina ignored the fear that she let her mother down and urgently yelled to Angela, "Ma, ma, wake up."

Groggy, Angela answered in an annoyed tone, "What is it, Cathy?"

Without hesitating, and answering dramatically, Catholina responded, "Hurry, hurry. Anthony fell out of the window."

Hearing the news, Angela jumped out of the sofa bed, not sure whether she heard her oldest daughter correctly. With a stern, worried look on her face, Angela stared down Catholina and asked, "What did you just say?" Excited and worried, Catholina answered her mother promptly. "Anthony, he fell out of the window. He's outside on the ground holding his arm. I think he is really hurt." Rapidly grabbing her pants and a shirt to cover the underwear she was accustomed to sleeping in, Angela began getting dressed.

Very disturbed, rushing to put her clothes on and attempting to find out what happened, Angela inquired, "Cathy, how did this happen?" Feeling she let her mother down, and beginning to cry, Catholina answered, "I don't know." With her daughter following close behind her, now dressed and rushing down the stairs, Angela—continuing to inquire—asked angrily, What do you mean you don't know? Weren't you watching them?" In an effort to defend herself, Catholina responded, "I was taking a shower. I thought they were all still sleeping."

Once outside, Angela ignored everything Catholina was saying and hurried to her baby. With a frightened look on her face, she dropped to her knees and very carefully pulled Anthony's body towards her own. With a sigh of relief that he was still alive, Angela began to comfort Anthony. Instantly changing his feelings from frightened to sad, Anthony said softly, "I'm sorry, Mommy. I didn't mean it." With her youngest son cradled in her arms, Angela said in a comforting tone, "Don't worry, baby. Everything is going to be alright."

After a couple of minutes, Angela—now relieved—transformed back to an efficient state of mind. Still holding Anthony, she instructed her oldest daughter. "Cathy," she said. "Knock on Dominic's door and ask him to call an ambulance." Without saying a word, Catholina quickly adhered to her mother's request.

Having been out the night before, and wearing just shorts, it took Dominic a few moments to answer the door. With a confused look on his face, and a little disorientated, Dominic asked, "What's going on?"

Catholina, who was about to answer, was interrupted by Angela. "Dominic, please do me a favor. Call an ambulance for me. Anthony just fell out the window."

Eager to help, Dominic responded, "Sure, no problem. Is he alright?" Answering his concerns, Angela replied, "Yeah, I think so. But my phone just got shut off, and he needs to go to the hospital."

Now wide-awake, Dominic went back into his apartment and honored Angela's request. After putting on a shirt and using the bathroom, Dominic returned with a cup of coffee for Angela. Looking around and seeing the distressed faces of Angela's family, Dominic—referring to the ambulance—announced, "They'll be right here." Handing the cup of coffee in Angela's direction, Dominic—out loud for anyone to answer—asked inquisitively, "Is he okay? How'd this happen?"

A moment passed. The girls, looking in Dominic's direction, didn't answer. Volunteering the information, and pointing to the beam which held up the roof of the porch, Joseph Jr. responded. "We were playing Batman and Robin and Anthony wanted to slide down the pole." Disgusted by Joseph Jr.'s comment, Josephina angrily interrupted, "Liar!" Getting everyone's attention, Josephina, still upset, continued. "He didn't want to, Joey, you made him do it." Trying to keep the truth from coming out, Joseph Jr. lashed back. "Shut up, you don't know. You're the one who knocked him off with the broom." Defending herself right away, Josephina responded, "I was trying to save him, and I wouldn't have had to if you didn't lock the window." Unable to respond with anything else, Joseph Jr. just said, "Shut up. You don't know what you're talkin' about."

Becoming angry from the bickering, Angela ended it by saying, "Both of yous be quiet, yous are all punished."

As the paramedics carted Anthony and prepared to put him in the back of the ambulance, Angela looked towards her oldest daughter and instructed her, "Cathy, look after your brother and sister until I can call your Grandmother to come."

Catholina agreed by nodding her head yes.

Watching the ambulance as it left, and continuing to do so until it was out of sight, Catholina turned to her younger siblings with an extreme look on her face. Very upset, she demanded both of them to go to their respective rooms. Adhering to her sister's command, Josephina went right away. But being the stubborn brat that he was, Joseph Jr. resisted and said, "No, I ain't going to my room. I don't have to listen to you."

Fuming, and walking rapidly toward him, Catholina

threateningly demanded, "You better go to your room, Joey. I swear, as God is my witness, I will kick the everliving shit out of you. Because of you I'm gonna get into trouble."

Knowing that his older and bigger sister had him overmatched, Joseph Jr. began making his way to his room. While doing so, he began cursing her under his breath. Just as he reached the bottom step of the porch, Catholina rushed up behind him and gave him a swift yet violent kick in his buttocks. Still angry following her kick, Catholina—directing her remark at Joseph, Jr.—said, "Here, take that, asshole." Laughing at Catholina's action, Dominic trotted back into his apartment, as did some of the other neighbors looking on.

Fortunately for Anthony, he had only suffered a dislocated shoulder. Although the injury was not severe, it would prove to be significant in the years to come. As for Angela, after discovering the whole truth of the incident she decided that Joseph Jr. would no longer be able to play with Anthony unsupervised. Angela realized that Joseph Jr. was having a destructive influence over his little brother and wanted to keep Anthony out of future danger. Since the two got along so well, it would now be Josephina's responsibility to look after Anthony. The idea seemed logical at the time for a few reasons. Unlike Joseph Jr., Josephina was a very happy child and loved her baby brother dearly. Also, having Anthony following her around gave Josephina a strong sense of responsibility and boosted her self-esteem. Josephina, simple, but not stupid, had always been overshadowed by her older sister's accomplishments. Catholina was a straight-A student, number one in her class, and was always commended by everyone for how smart she was. Having Anthony as her responsibility, Josephina could now feel her more important. No longer was she only just a pretty face; Josephina was now in charge of someone.

Beside being logical , Angela's decision to put Josephina in charge of Anthony would work out for everyone. Finally some pressure was being removed from Catholina. Rather than always being the role model, Catholina could finally do more things a child of her age should have been doing. Knowing

Josephina would never do anything to intentionally hurt her little brother, Anthony would be more safe away from the destructive influence of his older brother.

However, nothing is ever picture-perfect. There would be one problem that did exist: Josephina herself was attracted to doing things she wasn't supposed to, some of which would prove to be very dangerous. It would be one of Josephina's favorite games that would lead to another near-fatal experience for Anthony.

One of the biggest rules Angela established for her children had been that under no circumstances were they allowed to leave the square block. This meant they could play around the corner but were not allowed to cross any streets. It was an important rule Angela set forth because of the lack of traffic enforcement in New York in the 1970s. Even though there were speed limits posted, they were rarely enforced. Drinking and driving was not the major offense it is today, and reckless driving was common. The New York City police were much too preoccupied with major crimes to worry about traffic violators. Angela was very strict when it came to the rules she set forth for her children. If she caught them breaking any of her rules, they would be severely disciplined. Disciplinary actions from Angela varied from beatings to extreme punishments, depending on the rule that was broken. Creative as well, Angela's punishments would usually fit the crime, so to speak. If one of Angela's kids were caught cursing, she would wash their mouth out with soap. If Angela caught one of her kids leaving the block, he or she would not be able to go out to play for a month. In just about every case, along with every punishment Angela handed down, she would usually inflict a spanking as well.

Along with Josephina having a free-spirited personality, she also liked living dangerously. Even with the knowledge of what would happen if she were caught disobeying any of her mother's restrictions, Josephina would still chance it. It wasn't her intention to be defiant or disrespectful. She just liked to see how much she could get away with without getting caught. One of the disadvantages of coming from a poor family is that the children sometimes commit negative acts to fulfill the empty gaps left by the lack of certain luxuries. In Josephina's case, she broke rules because she did not have anything else to do. She had no toys to play with, no books to color, and the only games she could play were the ones she made up by her own imagination. That included her favorite game, "Ringing Doorbells and Running." Being significant, the game would lead to Anthony's next childhood trauma.

The rules to the game "Ringing Doorbells and Running" were simple. Each player had to choose a different house to work on. He would then ring the doorbell. Before the occupant answered, he would then run and hide in a place where he could observe. The occupant, usually with a baffled look on his face, caused much amusement for the kids watching from their respective hiding places — cars, trees, or bushes. The object of the game was to see how many times you could get a person to answer his or her door. The average was about three. After the third time, the occupant usually realized what was happening and just didn't answer any more. The player who made a person answer the most won the game. The record, set by none other than Josephina, was eight. It seemed only right that Josephina held the record, since she herself invented the game. Just about every time the game was played, Josephina would win. As it turned out, the only time Josephina ever lost was the last time it would be allowed to be played. The termination of the game came about due to the near-tragedy that occurred during play.

One hot summer day, the neighborhood kids decided to go out and play Ringing Doorbells and Running. Usually only four or five kids were willing to play. When there is only that many, it is every man for himself. On this particular day, there were more kids than usual willing to play — ten in all. Since there were that many kids, it was decided to make up five teams of two. Josephina, now responsible for her younger brother, of course teamed up with him. Also, because of the extra players, there were not enough houses on the block to go around. Therefore, Josephina decided to pick a house across the street. After all the other teams picked their houses, the game began.

The first team, consisting of Josephina's best friend, Lisa, and her little sister, Michelle, was able to make their victim answer three times. The second team, neighbors Tommy and Jennifer, were able to get their house to answer an astonishing six times. After they were finshed, it was Josephina and Anthony's turn.

Josephina rang, hid, and looked on. Of course the lady home answered the first time. She looked around, saw nobody, and went inside.

Josephina then sent Anthony. Anthony rang, ran and hide, then looked on. Once again the lady came out, looked around, and went in.

The third time, on Josphina's turn, the lady—now realizing the joke—opened her door slightly then retreated into her house.

Realizing that she might lose her own game for the first time, Josephina turned to her brother and said, Anthony, she is not going to fall for it again. You gotta do it differently. Instead of ringing the bell, knock on the door. Okay?"

Without argument, and having complete trust in his sister, Anthony nodded his head yes.

As he approached the house, Anthony noticed that the second door—which was made up of wood and behind the first door, which was all glass—was halfway open. It occurred to Anthony that, if he did not do it fast enough, the lady would see him from inside her house. Very quickly, Anthony ran to the house, knocked on the glass door, then ran and hid.

When the lady did not respond, Josephina arose from her hiding place and motioned to all the other players. Placing her hands together in the international sign for time-out, Josephina claimed, "Time-out, that didn't count. He didn't do it hard enough."

The other players, having complete respect for her and her game, did not object to Josephina's claim. Retreating back to their respective hiding places, everyone allowed Anthony to knock again.

Determined to win, Josephina pulled Anthony aside for

a pep talk. Grabbing him by the shoulders, then looking him in the eyes, Josephina—coaching, not demanding—said softly, "Look, Anthony, you know I love you, and I'm not gonna hurt you, but if we lose I am gonna be really upset." In an effort to please Josephina, a worried Anthony asked, "What should I do?" Releasing Anthony's arms and wiping the sweat from his forehead, Josephina answered, "Don't be afraid. All you have to do is knock on the glass a little harder. Use a rock if you have to. Okay? Are you ready?" With a little less fear than on his previous attempt, Anthony answered, "Yeah, I'm ready."

Kissing Anthony on the cheek and patting him lovingly on his buttocks, Josephina pointed him in the direction of the house and retreated to her hiding place.

Following the advice of his older sister, Anthony chose a medium-sized rock from the street and proceeded to approach the lady's house. All the fear that left Anthony's stomach while he was in his sister's arms had now returned. As he got closer to the door, Anthony's heart began beating faster and faster. With rock still in hand as he reached the bottom step of the porch, still walking slowly and stealthily, Anthony raised his right arm half-mast. With the overwhelming fear becoming too much for him, Anthony—in an instant, and without realizing what he was doing or the consequences of his next action—threw the rock that was now blistering in his hand. Even though it had only taken a split second from the time the rock left his hand for it to shatter the door he was only supposed to knock on, to Anthony it seemed as though the rock traveled through the air in slow motion. The sound of the shattering glass door seemed to be the only sound in the whole neighborhood. Once what just had happened registered in Anthony's mind, he quickly turned around to seek guidance from Josephina. With a look of horror on his face and his arm still raised half-mast, as though he were still holding the rock, Anthony watched everyone , including Josephina, quickly scatter away. Feeling scared and stranded—especially by the person he looked up to the most—Anthony only had two choices. He could wait there and accept responsibility for what he had done, or he could run and try to escape any and all disciplinary actions that awaited him. Considering Angela only had enough money to supply her children with only the bare necessities, if she had to pay to replace a window that one of her children had broken the punishment would be unimaginable. With that in mind, Anthony, needless to say, followed his instinct, and just like the others he ran like hell.

As Anthony made his daring escape, his first move was to get back across the street to his own block. With only escape on his mind as he ran into the street, Anthony neglected to check if any cars were coming in either direction. It would never be determined if the driver would have been able to stop his 1957 Chevy in time if he hadn't been speeding. Driving twenty miles an hour over the speed limit may or may have not been a factor in whether he hit Anthony. The manner in which Anthony darted out into the street would have made stopping difficult for the safest driver in the world. Being only ten feet from the point of impact, it is amazing the driver was able to slam on his brakes at all. Nevertheless, the speed of the car would be a factor in the extent of Anthony's injuries. Maybe if the car had been traveling at the correct speed, Anthony would have flown only ten feet instead of thirty. Hence the force would not have been as hard when Anthony slammed into the ground. If that had been the case, the doctors would have been able to save Anthony's kidney instead of having to remove it.

Immediately following Anthony's crash landing, the whole neighborhood rushed to the scene where the accident took place. Considering where the car was and where Anthony landed, and the blow to his head having knocked him unconscious, it was everyone's conclusion that Anthony was dead. A few minutes later, when the driver of the vehicle went to check on him, Anthony awoke. Not realizing that anyone else was watching, Anthony looked up at the driver hovering over him. Following his first instinct, he attempted to get up and run away. But as he attempted to do so, he was met by Marco. Marco was Tommy and Jennifer's father, two of the other kids playing the infamous game prior to the accident. Marco had stormed out of his house when his two children came running in after the Anthony had broken the window. Being as he was the first to reach Anthony after the driver of the vehicle, Marco heard the screech of the car and then saw Anthony fly.

Seeing a boy he had assumed dead trying to get up and run away, Marco couldn't believe his eyes when he reached Anthony. Right as Anthony made his daring attempt to escape, Marco grabbed him and lifted him up into his arms. With an amazed look on his face, Marco asked, "Where you going?"

Stunned and disoriented, Anthony hesitated to answer. After everything that had just transpired over the last few minutes, all Anthony could think about was how much trouble he would be in. As he came to, Anthony began to think about how angry his mother was going to be at him for crossing the street, breaking the glass, and getting hit by a car. As all these things ran through his mind, Anthony began to cry. Not from sadness or pain, the tears were from his terror of his mother's reaction.

As Marco carried him out of the street and away from further danger, Anthony replied, "I gotta go home." Making his way past all the accumulated onlookers who followed him as he passed, Marco replied, "Don't worry, I'm taking you." Even the lady whose window Anthony broke, whom everyone had forgotten about by now, followed along out of concern for the boy's condition.

When Marco reached Anthony's home, he found Catholina and Josephina sitting on the porch. Having gone into hiding after Anthony had broken the window, Josephina didn't know what had just happened. Her first thought was that Marco had caught Anthony and was going to tell their mother.

Speaking in the direction of the girls, but not specifically at either one of them, Marco asked, "Where is your mother?" In an effort to protect her little brother from being ratted on, Josephina answered, "She's not here. Why?"

Before Marco had a chance to respond, Catholina interrupted. "What happened?"

Knowing Angela would never leave her children home by

themselves, and realizing Josephina was lying, this time Marco addressed Catholina directly, "Please go get your mother. Anthony was just hit by a car." Worried, and without responding, Catholina dashed upstairs to get her mother. In the background one could hear Catholina's frantic voice saying, "Ma, ma, come quick. Anthony was hit by a car." Meanwhile, feeling the guilt of leaving her little brother, Josephina became hysterical. Within seconds, Angela was downstairs. As she approached Marco, who was holding Anthony, Josephina—still crying and standing in her mother's path—pleaded with her. "Mommy, I'm sorry; it was all my fault."

Angela, however, did not acknowledge Josephina. Instead she pushed her aside and attended to Anthony.

While taking Anthony from Marco's arms into her own, Angela asked into the crowd, "Did anyone call an ambulance?" Not a moment after Angela asked, a police car pulled up. From a nearby payphone, the driver of the vehicle which struck Anthony had called 911 immediately after the accident. Because of the incident just a year before, being carted off to the hospital wasn't a new or scary experience for Anthony. Up until the police car entered his sight, Anthony had been relatively calm. But when he saw the policemen get out of their car and make their way toward him, Anthony began to panic. Convinced he was about to go to jail, he grabbed his mother as tightly as he could and buried his face in her shoulders. Anthony had disobeyed his mother's rules and the cops were coming to take him away. It is not at all surprising that Anthony would think this way. Many times parents tell their children that if they are bad the police will come and arrest them. Besides, just a year before there wasn't any police presence when Anthony needed to go to the hospital.

Feeling Anthony tremble in her arms, and trying to console him by rubbing his back, Angela said softly, "Relax, baby. It's going to be alright." As he observed the cops begin to get closer, Anthony was terrified that he would never see his family again and attempted to squirm out of his mother's arms. Holding her baby more firmly now, Angela said, "Anthony, relax.

Where are you going?" Continuing to try to get away, Anthony pleaded, "Let go. Please let go. I'm sorry. I don't want to go to jail." Still worried, half a smile developed on the serious face of Angela. As she was about to explain to him the real reason why the cops were there, Anthony interrupted. "No, please no. I'm sorry; I won't do it again." A little annoyed now, yet still compassionate, Angela—referring to the two policemen now standing next to her—demanded, "Anthony, take it easy. They're not going to take you to jail." Relieved, and no longer trying to escape, Anthony inquired, "Why are dey here den? Where is da ambalints?" Before Angela could answer her son, the first cop—seeming to be the lead officer of the two—interrupted. "Don't worry, little man," he said. "We're not taking you to jail. You were in an accident. The police always come when there is an accident." More professionally than the first cop, the second added, "The ambulance is on the way." Much calmer yet still skeptical, and keeping his eyes on the policemen, Anthony put his arms around his mother and rested his head on her shoulder. Noticing that Anthony was distressed, the first cop turned to the second and instructed him, "Fred, why don't you start filling out the report?" Nodding his head yes, yet having a look on his face like he didn't know what to do, Fred just stood there waiting for more instructions. Noticing his partner's confused look, the first cop added, "You should probably start by taking the statement from the driver." Fred respectfully replied, "Yes, sir." Walking away and getting about ten feet, Fred was stopped by the first cop once again. Adding more instructions, the first cop said, "Fred." Halting, then turning around quickly, Fred responded, "Sergeant?" Making sure that his partner covered everything, the sergeant added, "Also get statements from any witnesses, okay? Thanks." Once again Fred answered obediently. "Yes sir." After which, Fred proceeded to carry out his orders.

Trying to reduce the built-up stress, the sergeant flirtingly said to Angela, "We just spoke to them on the radio, and like my partner said, the ambulance should be here any minute." Gratified for his help, Angela—rocking her baby in her arms—said to the sergeant, "Thank you so much." Attempting to keep them calm while waiting, the sergeant introduced himself by saying, "I'm sergeant John Rizzuto, and that was my partner, officer Fred Taylor." Freeing up her hand to shake his, Angela responded courteously. "Angela Pagano, nice to meet you." After which, sergeant John extended his hand towards Anthony and said, "Who is this little guy?" Not responding and rejecting the sergeant's handshake, Anthony turned his head away and buried his face in his mother's neck. Embarrassed by her son's rudeness, Angela responded, "I'm sorry, sir. This is Anthony. He is just being shy." Not seeming to be offended in any way, Sergeant John replied, "Quite alright. He had a rough day." Then putting his face to where Anthony could see him, Sergeant John added, "Didn't you, buddy?" Not amused by the sergeant at all, Anthony still refused to respond. Still embarrassed, Angela once again said apologetically, "I'm sorry, sir. He must be scared. He usually is not this rude." Sergeant John then insisted, "No, don't apologize, it's okay. By the way, you can call me John."

Even as a mother of four, Angela was always able to maintain her figure. As many men did when they met her, Sergeant John attempted to flirt with her. Beating around the bush to find out Angela's marital status, Sergeant John asked Angela, "Did anyone inform Mr. Pagano of the situation?"

Realizing the sergeant's intention, and finding it in poor taste that he would be trying to pick her up at this moment, Angela answered, "Yeah, of course he knows. He's my husband." Fortunately, right at the same moment the Sergeant was about to lay his best line on Angela, the ambulance arrived. As soon as the ambulance halted, Angela rolled her eyes at sergeant John, spoke politely yet untruly, and said, "Thank you, I gotta go now." After which, Angela and Anthony left right away for the hospital.

About ten minutes later, Angela and Anthony arrived at the emergency room of the hospital. Regardless of how many people were waiting before them, Anthony went right in to see the doctor. In most cases, childhood injuries are generally a priority in most emergency rooms. With Anthony now admitted into the examination room, Dr. Adams—coincidentally the physician who treated Anthony a year earlier—was the same doctor this time as well. With everyone remembering the last incident, Dr. Adams—playing surprised in an attempt to break the ice—said to Anthony, "Hello there. Back so soon?" Relieved to see a familiar face, Anthony smiled and said, "Hi. I got hit by a car." "You did?" asked the doctor. Very friendly and comfortable, Anthony replied, "Yeah." Not approving, Dr. Adams asked sarcastically, "What happened? Did you think playing in the street was safer than playing on the roof?" Not realizing the doctor asked the question jokingly, Anthony responded, "No, it was an accident." As he began to check out Anthony's injuries, the doctor replied, "Oh, I see. Does anything hurt?" Anthony pointed to the left side of his lower back and answered, "It hurts here." With a concerned look on his face, Dr. Adams turned to Angela and said, "There doesn't seem to be any broken bones. We'll have to take some x-rays to make sure everything else is alright." Understandingly, Angela agreed. Remembering the procedures from the incident the previous year, and referring to the statement the doctor just made to his mother, Anthony asked, "I'm goin to da piture room?" Pleased by his cooperation, Dr. Adams, smiling, replied, "That's right. You remember the picture room, don't you?" Remembering in detail the fact that stood out the most, Anthony replied, "Yeah, I have to be naked."

After the numerous test and x-rays were completed, it was discovered that the blow Anthony's left kidney sustained when he slammed into the ground caused severe damage. Having developed a blood clot, the kidney could no longer function correctly. It could take blood in, but was not be able to send it back out. Dr. Adams explained that as the blood from Anthony's body continued to circulate to the damaged kidney, it would eventually overinflate. Then, like a balloon with too much air, the kidney would explode inside of him. Determined therefore that his kidney needed to be removed right away, Dr. Adams instructed the nurse to prepare Anthony for surgery immediately. In the meantime, while Anthony was being prepped for surgery, and time being a factor, Dr. Adams could only briefly discuss the situation with Angela.

Without going into detail, Dr. Adams informed Angela, "Mrs. Pagano, I'm afraid we are going to have to operate on Anthony right away." Becoming rapidly terrified, Angela asked, "Why? What happened?" Urgently Dr. Adams explained, "Unfortunately, we do not have enough time to go into detail about Anthony's condition. All I can say is that there is an existing problem with one of your son's kidneys, and we are going to have to remove it." Concerned and deeply disturbed, Angela asked the doctor as he was walking away, "Is he going to be alright?" Turning back towards Angela but walking slowly away from her towards the operating room, Dr. Adams responded, "Yes, it's a common procedure. However, we have to do it now before it is too late." Looking at the fear in Angela's face, the doctor quickly added, "Don't worry, Mrs. Pagano. He'll be fine. The nurse has some release forms for you to sign, then she'll fill you in on the rest." Turning around and walking faster towards the operating room, Dr. Adams said to Anthony, "Just have a seat there and try to relax. The nurse will be right with you."

Shortly afterward, just as the doctor had indicated, the nurse appeared with Anthony's chart and a release authorization letter for Anthony's operation. Angela filled out all the paperwork as the nurse explained what was happening. Afterward Angela asked, "How long will it take him to heal?" Answering with instructions, the nurse responded, "If all the restrictions are followed, approximately three months." Quickly protesting, Angela asked, "He has to be in the hospital for three months?" Attempting to make it clearer, the nurse responded, "No, no, we'll only keep him here for a few weeks for observation. After that you can monitor him at home." Open to all the information, Angela asked, "What do I have to look for?" Being very specific, the nurse answered, "With Anthony only having one kidney to take on the work of two, he will be urinating blood until the remaining kidney becomes accustomed to the extra job." Very interested, Angela asked, "Does this mean when he doesn't urinate blood anymore he is fine?" Still specific, the nurse said, "No. We will release him when there is no longer steady blood in the urine. However, for the next three months or so, you will still see blood in his urine the first time Anthony uses the bathroom in the morning. When that doesn't happen anymore, then he is fine." Inquiring what else she could do, Angela asked, "What can I do to make sure Anthony heals on schedule?" Continuing to try and be very helpful, the nurse responded, "The most important and the most difficult thing is try and keep Anthony inactive. The more he runs around, and the more rough play he is engaged in, the longer it will take for him to heal."

Rolling her eyes, Angela said, "How do I keep a little boy inactive?" Smiling and agreeing, the nurse replied, "I have two boys of my own." Angela stressfully replied, "Oh, yeah, I have four kids altogether, and it's going to take all the strength God gave me to keep this kid from playing. Okay, keep him inactive. What else should I do?" Referring to some papers she was holding in her hand, the nurse responded, "Follow this diet for Anthony. These foods will strengthen his kidney and help it heal a little bit more quickly." Angela accepted the instructions and waited helplessly for the completion of Anthony's operation.

After a couple of hours, the operation successfully completed, Anthony was taken to his room, where he would be spending the next three weeks. By this time most of Angela's family had arrived at the hospital to lend their support. Still groggy from the operation and hooked up to numerous machines, Anthony did not respond to any of the company present. Supporting and advising her, everyone remained with Angela until visiting hours were over. Angela, reluctant to leave her baby alone, pleaded with the hospital staff to let her stay the night. Unfortunately, though, the hospital would not allow it. Anthony did not have a private room. Angela was told that if she stayed, it would not be considerate to the other patients who occupied the room with Anthony. Because of the hospital's policy, Angela's brother, Gerald, promised to drive her back first thing in the morning.

When Anthony awoke the next morning, he noticed he

was alone. It took a few minutes to register in Anthony's mind where he was and what was going on. Even though this was not the first time Anthony experienced a painful injury which landed him in the hospital, it was, however, scary for him—it being the first time he actually had to be there overnight. Anthony's last incident, falling off the roof and dislocating his shoulder, allowed him to be out the same day. When Anthony awoke the day after that accident, he was in his own bed, in his own house, and only had a sling on his arm. This time was entirely different. This time Anthony woke up with the following images: one, he was in a strange bed; two, on both sides of him were two other beds occupied by people he had never seen before; three, there were two large needles stuck into his arm, each having a tube connected to it, which led to a pouch on a stand next to him. One pouch contained a clear fluid, and the other contained what appeared to be blood. After analyzing all of these things, the fear in Anthony's heart was so overwhelming that when he tried to scream for help he could make no sound. Observing Anthony, and noticing he was scared to death, Tino, an eighteen-year old in the bed to the right of Anthony, instructed his little roommate, "Just push that button and the nurse will come."

Anthony, still extremely frightened, did not respond and just stared at the teenager nervously for a couple of minutes. Attempting to relax Anthony, Tino—stuttering a bit but in an assuring voice—said, "Don't worry, kid. Nobody is gonna hurt you here. If you want somethin, just push that button and the nurse will come and give it to you." Still hesitant to respond to Tino, Anthony did what he instructed and pushed the green button next to his bed.

Tino, an adolescent of Puerto Rican descent, wore his hair long according to the times and was exceptionally friendly to Anthony. Relieved that he had someone else to talk to, other than the other occupant of the room, Tino tried to make Anthony feel very comfortable. It wasn't that Tino disliked the other occupant of the room, it was just that the other occupant was in his nineties and was about to die at any moment.

Attempting to make friends with little Anthony, Tino

asked, "What's your name?" Holding on to the green button that he was instructed to push, Anthony replied, "Anthony." Continuing his introduction, Tino added, "Nice to meet you, Anthony, my name is Tino." Because of Anthony's Spanish-looking appearance, Tino, making the mistake that many did, asked, "Come sta hoy?" Which means, "How are you today?" in Spanish. Having the brown hair and eyes, the dark skin, full lips, and even the body structure, Anthony would always appear to be of Spanish descent. Tino, believing Anthony was Spanish, asked "Don't you understand Spanish?" Not trying to be rude, yet correcting Tino, Anthony said, "No, I'm Italian."

A little embarrassed by his mistake, Tino shrugged his shoulders and said, "So what? That's the same thing." A little nervous still, Anthony informed him, "This button don't work." Smiling and finding his lack of patience amusing, Tino said, "Wait a few minutes, these people are slow around here. They'll come, though." Continuing to befriend Anthony, Tino inquired, "What happened to you?" Becoming more relaxed now, Anthony replied, "I got hit by a car." Seeing how long he would have his new roommate, Tino asked, "Are you gonna be here for awhile?" Shrugging his shoulders because he didn't know the answer, Anthony replied, "I don't know. I thought I was home already, but then I woke up here." In the meantime, the conversation was interrupted when a nurse entered the room.

Looking at his chart, the nurse asked Anthony, "Is everything alright?" Attempting to find out the most important information at the moment, Anthony asked, "Where is my mommy?" Looking at her watch and noticing it was only 8:30 in the morning, the nurse answered, "I'm sure she will be here shortly. It is still early and visiting hours don't start until 10:00." Disappointed, Anthony gestured for the nurse to come closer to him ,and whispered, "I have to pee."

Closing the curtain around his bed for privacy, the nurse gave Anthony a bedpan and said, "Go in here." Never seeing one of these before, a puzzled Anthony inquired, "What is this?" Explaining briefly, the nurse responded, "This is your bathroom. Do you want me to show you how to use it?"

His face turning red from embarrassment, Anthony—unable to speak—just nodded his head yes. Smiling, the nurse proceeded to help Anthony.

Lifting him onto the bedpan in a seated position, then referring to his penis, the nurse instructed Anthony, "Just hold it down in there and go. I'll turn around. Just tell me when you're finished." Anthony did everything the nurse instructed all the way down to alerting her when he was finished. After which Anthony sat there quietly, still embarrassed as the nurse emptied the bedpan into the toilet, cleaned it out, and returned it back to the side of Anthony's bed.

Once he was done, the nurse asked Anthony, "You think you will be able to do this by yourself next time?"

Without speaking, Anthony nodded his head yes. Opening the curtain around his bed, the nurse added, "Well, if you need help, just push that green button like you did."

Ready to continue their conversation, Tino was now sitting up in his bed. Referring to Anthony using the bedpan, Tino jokingly asked, "Was that your first time?"

Not answering his question, Anthony just smiled. Becoming comfortable with Tino and changing the subject, Anthony asked, "What happened to you?" Reluctant to answer but doing so anyway, Tino replied, "I overdosed on heroin." Having no idea what Tino was talking about, Anthony asked, "What is overdosed on heroin?" Realizing he was talking to a little kid, Tino displayed the track marks on his arms to Anthony and said, "This is heroin." Nodding his head yes like he understood, Anthony said, "Oh yeah, my brother Joey had that once, but my mommy called him chicken pots." Avoiding further disclosure, Tino just smiled and acted as if his new little friend was correct. Curious about Tino's situation, Anthony asked, "Is your mommy coming too?" Saddened by Anthony's question, Tino responded, "No, they ain't comin'. They're all mad at me for what I did." Noticing Tino's sadness and quickly attempting to console him, Anthony said, "Don't worry, they will come. When Joey had the heroin, my mommy made us stay away from him too, because it's catchy. But when he was better, we were allowed to play with him again. So when you're better, your family will come back too." Even though Anthony did not really know what was happening with him, Tino realized that in his small way the kid had a point.

Feeling hopeful now, Tino smiled and said, "Thanks, Anthony. You're right; my family will see me again when I'm better." Getting off the subject and needing to kill time, Tino asked, "Hey, Anthony, you want to watch TV?"

Although each bed had its own television set, the hospital charged ten dollars a day to have it turned on. Since Anthony's television was not turned on yet—and because of Angela's financial situation it probably wouldn't be, either—as soon as Tino asked him to watch his, Anthony immediately answered, "Yes." Positioning the television so that both beds could view it, Tino asked, "What do you want to watch?" While Tino was flicking the knob on the television, Anthony quickly replied, "I want to watch cartoons." Laughing aloud, Tino responded, "Why did I even ask? Cartoons it is."

Afterward the two roommates watched TV until visiting hours began and Anthony's family arrived.

The first week of Anthony's hospital stay was very exciting for him. Just about everyone Anthony had ever known in his short life came to visit. Best of all, nobody showed up empty-handed, and unlike Christmas and his birthday, Anthony actually received gifts that he enjoyed. If he only knew that getting hurt would bring so many toys into his life, Anthony would have done so a long time ago. For the first couple of days, the visitors were mainly family members. The friends of the Pagano family all visited the remainder of Anthony's first week. Even Joseph Sr. came one day. Anthony did not recognize him at first, and even though he showed up drunk and empty-handed, Anthony was still happy to see his father. Considering that the rest of Angela's family did not want him there, the visit by Joseph Sr. was quite short. Neglecting to bring even a get-well card for his son, Joseph Sr. did, however, agree to pay the hospital the ten dollar fee so that Anthony could watch television for one day.

After that one-day visit, Anthony would not see him again for about twenty-five years.

Unlike the first, the following two weeks for Anthony began to go downhill. Tino was discharged. Then, shortly thereafter, the old man in the bed to the left of Anthony dropped dead one day trying to make it to the bathroom. All of a sudden Anthony was alone his room. Up until she could no longer find babysitters for her other three children, Anthony's only consistent visitor was his mother Angela. If being all alone and immobilized in a hospital room wasn't enough to traumatize a little boy, the next turn of events surely would. It would be the next experience that would introduce Anthony to evil for the first time. The experience would also affect Anthony's outlook on life forever.

Toward the end of Anthony's second week in the hospital, he had become very restless from the boredom of just lying in his hospital bed. There wasn't much to keep Anthony busy, and the visitations had become less frequent to just about scarce. On that Friday, as soon as visiting hours began at 10:00 in the morning, Miss Evans paid a visit. Miss Evans was the third grade teacher in the children's school. As Miss Evans entered his room, Anthony's face lit up. The child, alone in his room and bored to death, finally had someone to keep him company. Although Anthony was not that fond of the estranged teacher, he was open and friendly to her. Miss Evans, a buxom yet petite woman in her early thirties, had been Anthony's only visitor for a couple of days now. Having short blonde hair and blue eyes, Miss Evans was not married; neither did she have any children of her own.

Having become a teacher because of her love for children, Miss Evans had always liked Anthony very much. Whenever she saw him, she would literally drop whatever she was doing to give him a hug and kiss. Always giving him extra attention, Miss Evans would always compliment Anthony on his appearance as well. It was no secret that this young woman adored Anthony. Waiting for the perfect moment, which seemed to be now, it was, however, a secret what Miss Evans' intention for Anthony was.

As she entered the room, Miss Evans greeted Anthony with a big hug and kiss, as she usually did. Unaware of her plans, Anthony accepted Miss Evans' affection while she gave him a second kiss, this time on the lips. Wearing a low-cut blouse and a miniskirt, Miss Evans sat on Anthony's bed with her body next to his and her arm draped around his waist. Leaning in close so that Anthony could see her cleavage, Miss Evans looked him in the eyes and asked, "How are you feeling, baby?" Nervous because of the manner in which the teacher positioned herself, Anthony responded, "Okay, but I wish I could leave now." Looking around to see if anyone was watching, Miss Evans began to caress Anthony's head and said, "Poor baby. Are you homesick?"

Now looking and noticing that the green button to call the nurse was out of his reach, Anthony responded, "Yeah, it's very boring in here. I have nothing to do and no one to play with."

Continuing to caress him, working her hand from his head to his shoulders and chest, Miss Evans said, "That's okay, sweetheart. I'll play with you. I have a real good idea for a game we can play too." Excited from her response, Anthony quickly questioned, "What?"

Guessing that Anthony would be bare underneath his hospital gown, Miss Evans began to stroke Anthony's lower stomach with her fingernails and pull up his medical gown. Getting up from the bed momentarily, and pushing the call button for the nurse even further out of reach, Miss Evans said, "We are going to have to close these curtains." As Miss Evans proceeded to close the curtains around his bed, Anthony asked defensively, "Why do you have to close da curtins?" Being very convincing, and tricking Anthony, Miss Evans explained, "Because this is a secret game that only grown-ups can play. But since you need to cheer up, I am going to play it with you."

Nervous yet curious, Anthony asked, "How do you play? What do I do?" As she made her way back to his bed, Miss Evans replied, Nothing. Just close your eyes and I'll do everything."

After Anthony closed his eyes, Miss Evans began to get bolder. She started to run her hands slowly up his legs. Feeling uncomfortable and flinching about, Anthony asked, "Miss Evans, what are you doing?" Obviously not new at seduction, the disturbed teacher responded, "Don't worry, baby, this is all just part of the game."

Confused and helpless, Anthony let out a breath and then closed his eyes again. Once his eyes were closed, Miss Evans proceeded to run her hands up his legs, this time a little further than before. After her hands reached their ultimate goal, Miss Evans moved her body towards Anthony until his face was level with her breast. In an attempt to arouse her victim, Miss Evans began to whisper sensually into Anthony's ear and said, "Ooh, you're not wearing any underwear. That's okay, neither am I."

Anthony tried to close his eyes even harder. As Miss Evans fondled his penis, Anthony became erect. Holding his penis and feeling the heat increase in her hand, Miss Evans—becoming excited and beginning to moan—said, "That's it, baby. This is how you play this game. Let's see how strong you are."

Pinned down, unable to speak or resist, Anthony's heart began to race. Even though the teacher, whom he was taught to always respect and obey, insisted that this was just a game, Anthony couldn't help but be frightened. Feeling his erection was complete, Miss Evans, encouraging him, said, "Wow, Anthony, you are very big for your age. I know some grown men who aren't even this big." These words may have made a grown man feel good, but to Anthony they meant nothing. Anthony, on the other hand, just couldn't wait until this game was over. Just as what he was experiencing was not about to end any time soon, the memory of this game would stick in Anthony's mind forever. Selfish in nature, Miss Evans continued her sin and mounted Anthony. Guiding him inside, Miss Evans took Anthony's only free hand and forced him to touch her. Miss Evans was delicate no longer. Her intention to get-off, she became very rough with her subject until she was finished. With Anthony terrified and crying, Miss Evans put her lips onto his, forced her tongue in his mouth, and removed herself from his body. Afterwards, Anthony immediately looked down towards his groin. One can only imagine what went through

Anthony's mind while watching his crazed teacher have an orgasm. Seeing her scream as she did, then feeling the hot, wet discharge all over his pelvic area, Anthony must have thought that Miss Evans had broken his penis. Observing that Anthony was just about to yell out for the nurse, Miss Evans quickly covered his mouth and said, "Remember, Anthony, this was a secret game." With a terrified look in his eyes, Anthony tried to remove the lunatic's hand from his mouth, but unfortunately was unsuccessful. Only having one free hand, Anthony was no match for the vibrant teacher. Continuing to keep his mouth covered, Miss Evans pinned Anthony down until he was calm. Once she saw him surrender and begin to relax, Miss Evans—using intimidation—said, "Look, Anthony, I'm not going to hurt you. I have to explain something to you, but you can't say anything until I am finished. If I let go of your mouth, will you promise not to yell?"

Still terrified, yet willing to be obedient, Anthony nodded his head.

No longer being the sweet, loving lady that Anthony knew before, Miss Evans, removing her hand slowly from his mouth, began to talk demandingly to Anthony. Miss Evans started the conversation by saying, "Anthony, you know you can't tell anyone about this game we played, right?" Disgusted by Miss Evans and the coward she was, Anthony asked, "Oh yeah? Why not? Are you afraid you're gonna get in trouble?" Becoming agitated, Miss Evans convincingly explained, "No. I won't get in trouble. This was a grown-up game we played, and I am a grown-up. If anyone would get in trouble for playing, it would be you." Attempting to defend himself, Anthony said, "But you let me play." Using her mind to outsmart the boy, Miss Evans continued. "It doesn't matter that I let you play. Do you know what they do to little boys who play grown-up games?" Even though he did not have a choice, Anthony—feeling guilty about what he took part in—shook his head no. Attempting and succeeding to put enough fear in him to keep him quiet, Miss Evans continued, "They take the boy away from his mother forever, then put him in a room by himself just like this one. Then you'll never see your family again." Once Anthony heard that, whether it was true or not, he was not going to take the chance. Anthony detested being where he was, and was not about to do anything to keep that situation permanent.

Worrying about being taken from his home, Anthony asked, "What do I do? How do I keep them from finding out I played this game?" At ease now because she fooled the youngster, Miss Evans consoled him by saying, "Don't worry, Anthony. If you don't tell them, nobody will find out." With the classic sad puppy dog look on his face, Anthony inquired, "You won't say anything?" Just like she wanted to, Miss Evans realized she had Anthony right where she wanted him. Ensuring Anthony, Miss Evans replied, "Of course I won't say anything. This will be our little secret. If you want to play again when you are better and out of the hospital, we can do that too."

Relieved by Miss Evans' response, Anthony gratefully replied, "No, thanks. I don't like this game. Besides, I don't want to get caught." Then, very encouragingly, Miss Evans asked, "Are you sure? You are a very good player and you will get even better the more you play." Again, Anthony shook his head no and said, "Thanks, but I am not a grown up. I am really afraid to play this grown-up game." Still insisting, Miss Evans said, "You will like it more when you are better, I promise. Just think about it, okay?"

Confident that Anthony would not disclose the incident to any one, Miss Evans decided it was time to leave. Relieved by her departure, Anthony made no attempt to try to stop her. Anthony figured he was better off being by himself. Not knowing whether she had told the truth about the consequences he would face, Anthony decided it was best not to talk about the experience he had with the crazed teacher. Until this day, with the exception of two of the closest people to him, Anthony kept the incident a secret. Not being one of the two people he told, Angela would eventually die before ever finding out what happened to her baby in the time he was most vulnerable. Coaching him through some future rough times, Angela would never know what was behind Anthony's lifelong disturbance.

As for Miss Evans, eventually—as all child molesters do—I'm sure she got caught doing this to another child. It was evident that Anthony wasn't the first child Miss Evans had raped; and as bold as she was, surely Anthony wasn't the last. It is unfortunate that people like Miss Evans exist in the world. Only thinking about their own selfish needs, they don't realize the lifelong scars and damages their actions cause for others.

Miss Evans, however typical, wasn't what most people would have considered a typical rapist. During the era in which Anthony was molested, children in general were not taken seriously in such matters. Most adults would not believe a child when they spoke badly about another adult. The child would either be considered a liar or just mistaken.

Miss Evans was a young, attractive, and accomplished teacher. Adored by most parents, it would have been very difficult to believe that this highly-respected member of the community would commit rape. That was one of the dilemmas Anthony faced when he became old enough to realize what had really happened to him. It wasn't a game—a grown up game, like Miss Evans said. Anthony was a victim of a sick individual.

What makes a person want to do this to a child? I'm sure there are many reasons, but none of them would satisfy God or the victims that are involved themselves. In Miss Evans' case, it seemed to be a power thing. The simple fact that she took advantage of little boy when he was at his weakest demonstrates that she needed to be the person in control of a situation. Because of the cool demeanor she displayed, it can be determined that Anthony was not Miss Evans' first victim. Simply because of the small remorse she displayed afterwards, it is safe to say that Miss Evans would strike again. In almost every case, even after they get caught, child molesters usually never stop.

It is unfortunate that you cannot foresee a rape until after the actual act is committed. Even if the molester gets caught after just committing one act, he or she still altered somebody's life forever. This being the case, just imagine how many lives out there have already been affected. In Anthony's life, the effect of the experience would not begin to show until later on. Anthony's future sexual appetite would not be the same as that of a normal person. Even during his adolescent years, while all his peers were trying to conquer as many sexual partners as they possibly could, Anthony would isolate himself. In the relationships he did have, he would usually be the inferior one. Never being the one in control, Anthony would be the one who would have to please his partner, regardless of whether he were pleased in return. And because of the strict intimidation by which Angela ruled her household, it is possible Anthony would not be comfortable with any woman who could not control him in some way.

After Anthony was discharged from the hospital, Angela needed to make some changes. To keep them off the streets and out of trouble, particularly the boys, Angela concluded they needed more structure in their lives. Then, during Anthony's healing process, the last straw came for Angela.

As the doctor had instructed, Anthony was to stay inactive and avoid aggravating the side of his body from which the kidney had been removed. Unable to stand seeing his little brother happy, being the jealous bully that he was, Joseph Jr. was going to prove this easier said than done. One day while Anthony was playing with one of the many toys he received while in the hospital, Joseph Jr. came up to him and demanded, "Gimme that. I want to play with it." Very generously, Anthony hesitated when he responded, "One minute. I am almost finished with it. Then you can have it." Unsatisfied with his little brother's response and quickly becoming angry, Joseph Jr. said, "I don't care if you're finished or not. Gimme it now or else."

Trying to avoid any conflict, and without saying another word, Anthony turned away from Joseph Jr. to give him the toy he wanted. Believing that Anthony was going to disobey him, and finding that disrespectful, Joseph Jr. kicked Anthony with all his might in the already-injured part of his back and yelled, "That's what you get for ignoring me."

Unable to scream or even cry, Anthony stumbled out into the hallway holding his side. Walking out of her room at the same time, Catholina observed Anthony as he collapsed to the floor. As Joseph Jr. went to kick his little brother again, Catholina intervened by saying with a loud, disgusted voice, "Joey! What the fuck are you doing? What the hell do you want to do? Kill him?" Hearing her usually easygoing, proper daughter angry and cursing, Angela came storming out of the living room into the hallway. Noticing Anthony in pain on the floor, but addressing Catholina, Angela inquired, "What's going on here? Why are you cursing?" Defensive and very upset, Catholina replied, "Joey kicked Anthony in the back. He would have done it again if I didn't walk out of my room too." With one of those angry mother looks on her face, Angela instructed, "Cathy, go to your room." As she picked up her baby in an attempt to ease his pain, Angela took a deep breath and inquired, "Joey, is this true? Did you kick your brother? And you better not lie to me." Attempting to explain his reasoning, and only regretting getting caught, Joseph Jr. answered, "Yeah, but because he wouldn't share." Priority being to tend to Anthony, Angela calmly demanded, "Joey, go to your room." After putting Anthony down in the living room, Angela armed herself with a large wooden spoon and angrily made her way back to Joseph's room, where she beat him until the spoon broke. Even hurting from the beating, Joseph Jr., being the stubborn fool he was, giggled and said, "Good for you. Your weapon broke." Why on earth Joseph Jr. just didn't keep his mouth shut and take the beating, one could never understand. Maybe there was some kind of twisted reasoning behind his actions. Whatever it was, it didn't work. To make Angela more upset was the only thing Joseph Jr. accomplished. Walking away, and talking under her breath, Angela said, "You think that is funny, huh?" Not a moment later, Angela returned, armed this time with a heavy metal spoon. With more anger now, Angela continued where she left off and beat Joseph Jr. more violently. Each strike harder than the previous one, Angela swung that larger-than-life metal spoon over and over while saying, "Let's see you laugh at this. You are to never touch Anthony again, you hear me? Do you hear what I am saying to you?"

Although the beating Angela gave him was more severe than her regular ones, it would not teach Joseph Jr. a lesson. As long as the two boys existed, the older one would always bully the younger throughout their childhood. Finding alternative activities for the boys was the only hope Angela had to keep the peace. This would eventually bring on the very short athletic career of Anthony. In an effort to keep her boys apart, Angela went down to their church and signed Joseph Jr. up for the summer baseball league. Because of his injury, Anthony would not be able to sign up until the following year. For Joseph Jr., playing baseball was strictly recreational. Never really taking the game seriously, Joseph Jr. wasn't too upset when the league had to shut down.

But it was different for Anthony. The moment he stepped onto the ball field, he was a natural. Though excellent in hitting, throwing, and catching, Anthony's greatest talent was that he could run like the wind. Winning by far when put in a race against even some of the older kids in the league, none of the coaches ever saw anyone who could run as fast. As the years went on, Anthony developed into an extraordinary ballplayer. Every year, and for every team he played, Anthony was always an all-star and voted most valuable player. Because of his size and athletic ability, in the beginning Anthony was called on to be the catcher. Ever since his childhood injury in which he had dislocated his shoulder, Anthony had an extremely strong arm. Because Anthony's arm was so strong, the coach would end up switching him from catcher to pitcher. Not as great a pitcher as he was a catcher, many believed the switch took away from Anthony's game. Anthony's coach had only switched him because he was the only player on the team able to throw so hard. Being such an outstanding, all-around player, one year Anthony led his team to the state championship and then to nation's regional finals.

Then one year, in the summer before Anthony was to begin high school, as fast as it began, Anthony's baseball career was over. On one beautiful early-summer day, as the teams showed up to play their first game of the season, they all found was that their baseball field was deserted. As it turned out, the chairman of the Baseball League ran off and disappeared with the funds that would have allowed the church to provide baseball that year. Just as the church's baseball season ended before it got started, so did Anthony's hopes to ever play the game again. It wasn't that Anthony wanted to give his sport up; there were just no alternatives available for him. Anthony played for the church because it was free. The same would have been true for high school, but unfortunately the high school Anthony was zoned to attend did not have any sports available. The only way Anthony would have been able to play again was if someone were willing to pay for him to go to a special school. Although Angela could have found a way to pay for Anthony to attend such a school, she did not want to take the chance of wasting the money. She simply did not have enough faith in Anthony's abilities to believe that he could overcome the odds and pursue baseball as a career. However, we cannot read into this and blame Angela for Anthony's missed opportunities. She had no way of knowing how much money that even the worst professional athlete would eventually make. It wasn't Angela's fault that she had to work all the time to raise four kids by herself. Maybe if Angela had a day off, she would have been able to attend some of Anthony's games and see how good he actually was. Maybe if Anthony's father wasn't a drunken bum, and helped Angela financially, she wouldn't need to be so conservative and would have been able to roll the dice and pay for Anthony to go to that school.

In any event, Anthony would end up having to go to public school and look for an alternative career. Since his love for baseball was so strong, it was very difficult for Anthony to replace it. Subjects such as art and music only stimulated Anthony's mind. Unable to find any physical challenges, Anthony became restless. Simply because he could not find anything else he really wanted to do, Anthony began to believe he would never succeed in anything.

High school in general is a rough time in any teenager's life. Considering his background, it would prove exceptionally rough for Anthony. Even though both Josephina and Joseph Jr. were both attending the same school, neither wanted Anthony tagging along with them and their friends. To avoid being alone, Anthony began hanging around the only kids who would accept him for who he was. These kids, all of whom came from broken homes and poor families such as Anthony's, could more or less be defined as a gang. Calling themselves "The Mutts," the group was made up of kids from various ethnic backgrounds and all sorts of dysfunctions. From having alcoholic and drug-addicted to absentee parents, all the kids in the gang had at least one thing in common: They were considered misfits by the kids who came from good families. Every member of The Mutts had been underprivileged or deprived in one way or another. Only having each other to depend on, none of these kids ever had the luxury of being able to turn to their parents for money, or anything else for that matter. Also, because of their financial status, the gang was often called upon to defend their honor against some of the other kids in the neighborhood. In an effort to get some of the better things in life, many of the gang members found alternative, and unethical, means to make money. Doing anything from selling drugs, stealing cars, and even holding people up, it wasn't surprising that the kids who were financially secure picked fights with the members of The Mutts. Not understanding how it feels to be poor, and trying to keep their neighborhood decent, the richer kids did not want the gang to operate anything illegal around the neighborhood. Afraid that the values of their homes were going to be brought down, many physical confrontations were brought upon because of the conflict of interests. Each side having their own legitimate reason to stand their ground, nobody ever gave in. As long as all these different types of people lived in the same neighborhood, the friction would continue to exist as well. Eventually, the members of "The Mutts" who did survive, and didn't go to jail, would grow up, get jobs, and move on with their lives.

For Anthony, being a member of the gang brought on a lot of first-time experiences for him. With his hopes of becoming a baseball star now far behind, there was left an empty void inside that needed to be filled. Anthony first tried smoking, encouraged by his lifelong friend Vincent. Like Anthony, Vincent also had a father who had abandoned his family. The only difference in Vincent's case was that Vincent was already twelve when his father disappeared. Being, unlike Anthony, very close to his father, Vincent was severely traumatized after he left. Being a truck driver by trade, Vincent's father made a good living for his family. When his father was in the picture, Vincent was able to get anything he wanted. For Vincent it was an extremely tough adjustment after his father's departure. There is a big difference in being born poor, as opposed to becoming poor after already accustomed to being well off. Being almost the opposite of Angela, Vincent's mother, Regina, unlike Angela, was not very strict at all. She had no control over Vincent or his older sister, Maria. Vincent's father had always been the one to discipline the children. So having no respect for Regina, Vincent and Maria went completely wild after their father left.

Vincent and Anthony had been friends since the sandbox. Only a month apart in age, the two began playing together because Angela and Regina were best friends. Always attracted to danger, both Vincent and Anthony needed to be closely supervised when they were younger. With Vincent following him, Anthony was always looking for trouble. The first, but definitely not the last, example of this was when, at the age of four, Anthony talked Vincent into trying to flush each other down the toilet.

One hot summer day, their parents refusing to take them to the beach, Anthony came up with a most brilliant and crazy idea. Leading Vincent as he usually did, Anthony said, "I know how to get to the beach. It's a shortcut."

Very much wanting to go, and happy to hear this, Vincent asked, "Where?" Acting if he knew for sure, Anthony responded, "Well, if we flush ourselves down the toilet, it will take us to the ocean in the beach." For some reason—maybe because of their naïve age—this idea made a lot of sense to Vincent. Quickly agreeing, without asking any questions, Vincent replied, "Good idea, I'll go first." Obviously the two were not successful at their attempt. Coming out of the bathroom, both of them soaking wet, the only thing they had accomplished that day was pissing off their parents.

In most cases, it was Anthony who led Vincent into trouble. The only time the roles were ever reversed was when the two began smoking. Showing up one day with a pack of cigarettes he had stolen from his mother, it wasn't difficult for Vincent to talk Anthony into smoking. Both their parents being smokers, Anthony and Vincent did so without thinking there was anything wrong with it. Not even trying to keep it secret from his mother, Vincent actually began to smoke regularly once his father was out of the picture. Anthony, on the other hand, fearing his mother and never knowing what would ever be okay with her, kept everything he could from Angela. Always blaming his mother for his father leaving, Vincent felt the exact opposite of the way Anthony did. Vincent actually wanted Regina to know of his rebellious behavior. Since Regina let her appearance slide as she got older, Vincent believed that his father left because he was no longer attracted to his mother. Not employed, and rarely ever changing out of her nightgown, Regina became extremely overweight. With his mother smoking three packs of cigarettes a day and spending the majority of her day on the phone, it is understandable that Vincent would think as he did.

Only twelve years old, and doing it for different reasons, neither Anthony nor Vincent had ever smoked before that first time Vincent introduced it to Anthony. Vincent smoked to rebel, while Anthony did it to fill the empty void in his life. Chain-smoking one cigarette right after the other, Anthony became sick after he and Vincent had finished the pack. After a night of throwing up, only to smoke again the very next day, Anthony decided to do it differently. Learning from his mistake, Anthony the second time smoked only one cigarette each hour. In this way, Anthony began smoking on a regular basis. Contrary to his attempt, smoking would not fill the empty void in Anthony's life. As it turned out, beginning to smoke just opened up the door for Anthony to begin experiment with other things.

About six months later, on Mother's Day, Angela and

Regina were to be taken out to dinner by all the kids. In the early afternoon hours, while the girls were getting dressed, Catholina, now a young working class woman, approached Anthony and said, "Anthony, do me a favor. Go find Joey. We got to get ready to go now." Looking to get out of the house anyway, Anthony replied, "Okay, no problem." Requesting his company, Anthony turned to Vincent, who was sitting next to him in the living room, and said, "C'mon, go with me."

Hesitant to go because of his crush on Josephina, Vincent responded, "Na, I wanna stay here." Annoyed by Vincent's response, and referring to his now very attractive older sister, Josephina, Anthony asked again—more demandingly and convincingly—"C'mon Vinny. Let's go. I know why you want to stay here, but she's not even dressed yet. She's gonna be in the room doing her hair and make up forever. Besides, you're gonna see her all night." Rarely ever disagreeing with Anthony, Vincent as usual caved in and said, "All right, let's hurry up, though."

On their way now to find Joseph Jr., both of them lighting up cigarettes and referring to the members of the gang they were in, Anthony said, "Vinny, lets go to the schoolyard, see what the boys are doing." Being the local hangout for their gang, the "schoolyard" was also the back yard of the elementary school the kids attended. With Josephina still on his mind, Vincent answered, "Na, there is no time." Realizing where Vincent's answers were coming from, Anthony—becoming annoyed— replied, "Stop already. I told you you're gonna see her all night. Besides, Joey is probably there anyway." Without further resistance, Vincent followed Anthony. After about ten minutes of walking, Anthony and Vincent arrived at the schoolyard.

As they entered, neither Anthony nor Vincent were able to see anyone. However, the way the "schoolyard" was built—and what made it such a good hangout for the gang—there was a large incline that no one could see from the street or when someone first walked into the yard. On this incline were the back stairs that led into the the school. As Anthony and Vincent walked through the yard, they were able to hear voices and laughter in the near distance. Once they turned the corner of the indented part of the building, sure enough they found Joseph Jr. hanging out with some of the other gang members. While approaching, Anthony found this to be a little strange. Not only was Joseph Jr. not in the gang, he had also made it clear to Anthony that he didn't like any of them. Yet there he was, hanging out, laughing it up with Tommy, who was indeed a member of the gang. Around Joseph's age, a couple of years older than Anthony, Tommy made his money by selling marijuana out of that same schoolyard. This fact made it even stranger that Joseph was hanging out there. Until Anthony and Vincent got closer to him, Joseph didn't realize his little brother was approaching. All of a sudden it made sense to Anthony what Joseph Jr. was engaged in. Really unsure what to say, Anthony inquired, "Joey, what the fuck are you doin'?" Startled, yet not concerned, Joseph Jr. replied, "What does it look like?"

Looking towards Vincent, then back towards his brother, Anthony asked, "You're getting high?" Not to be shown up by his little brother, Joseph Jr. answered, "Yeah, so what? Why, you gonna tell mommy?" Interrupting and answering for him, Tommy said, "Na, he's no rat. He ain't tellin' nobody' nuttin'."

Confused about what he should do, Anthony had a tough decision to make right there. Looking around, Anthony felt as if everyone were staring at him. There was of course Joseph Jr.; Tommy; Vincent; another gang member, Miguel; and his younger sister, Juanita. Anthony only had two choices he could make—either one of them life-altering: the "After School Special" choice, the one where Anthony does the right thing— walking away and giving up the only people who accepted him and wanted him around; or the realistic choice. Living where he did and knowing what he knew, Anthony reacted as any other adolescent would have in that spot. Smiling and joking along, Anthony replied, "I won't tell if you pass me that joint."

There weren't too many kids who would have acted any differently in that spot. It was in the mid 1980s that Anthony smoked pot for the first time. During these times, there was not the major emphasis on drug use in the country as there is today. Rarely would one see anti-drug messages on television, nor did the federal government campaign to enforce the laws on illegal drugs. The crime rate in New York City was too high for police to pay any mind to drug users, and it wasn't strange to see the police cruise right past the kids smoking marijuana or drinking alcohol in the street. Also playing a big role in the movies, drugs were in a way socially acceptable. In truth, Anthony would have been considered strange if he hadn't chosen to smoke the marijuana right there.

After taking that first hit from the joint, Anthony did not feel any effect at all. Only taking one pull, Anthony quickly passed the joint to Vincent. Without hesitating, Vincent took the joint; and unlike Anthony, he took a few drags. Even though it was also Vincent's first time smoking marijuana, he was actually looking forward to it. Vincent was open to doing anything that he thought would upset his mother. As the joint came around again, Anthony heard the sweetest voice ever come from his left side say, "Wait, let me give you a shotgun."

The voice belonged to Juanita, the prettiest girl in the neighborhood, who was also a member of The Mutts. It caused Anthony to tremble where he stood. Curious, and also trying to look cool, Anthony replied, "Okay, sure. But what is the shotgun?" To Anthony's surprise, Juanita, taking a liking to him, responded, "I'll show you, but we have to do it in private, though."

Taking the joint from him and holding his hand, Juanita led Anthony away from the others to where they could no longer be seen.

Juanita put the joint in Anthony's mouth and said, "Close your eyes."

Remembering what happened the last time a woman told him to do that, Anthony asked, "Why? What are you gonna do?" Waiting a long time for this, Juanita insisted, "Don't worry. I promise I won't hurt you. I would never hurt you. Just trust me, okay? I promise you'll like it." That being said, Anthony did as Juanita instructed without further resistance.

With his eyes closed and the joint still in his mouth, Juanita put her arms on Anthony's shoulders and her mouth over the other end of the joint until her lips were touching his. In this position, Juanita began to blow smoke from the joint into Anthony's mouth. Overwhelmed by the inhalation, Anthony began to cough violently. Observing that this was too much for Anthony, Juanita regretfully said, "Oh my God, I'm so sorry, baby. Are you alright?" Still attempting to be cool, but at the same time disappointed, Anthony replied, "Why did you do that to me?" Thinking this was what he wanted, and becoming sad, Juanita replied, "I'm so sorry. I mean, I really am, Anthony. It's just that, well, I really like you. And I wanted you to like me. I figured after I sneaked you a kiss, you would. You know, like it happens in the movies." Pausing for a minute, and feeling bad that he snapped at her, Anthony replied, "Really? Well, then, I'm sorry too. And Juanita, I do like you, and I liked the kiss too. I just got mad because I thought you were playing a trick on me by blowing all that smoke in my mouth. But I'm sorry, I didn't know." In an effort to further explain her motives, Juanita replied, "No, I wasn't trying to do that. I wanted to get you to like me. Really. Please, Anthony, you have to believe me." Cracking a smile, and referring to the joint still in his hand, Anthony replied, "Look Juanita, it's okay. I believe you. Let me give this back to them, then I'll come back and we can talk." A little relieved now, Juanita happily asked, "Really? You're not mad at me?" Attempting to ensure her Anthony replied, "Na, don't worry about it. I'll be right back." Anxious, and not wanting Anthony to leave her sight, Juanita said, "Wait, Anthony. I'll go with you."

As they returned to the others, Anthony and Juanita received three different reactions. The first, out of the mouth of Joseph Jr., was "It's about time. Where's my weed?" While Anthony gave back the joint, Miguel teasingly asked his little sister, "Did you love birds have fun?" Turning red from embarrassment, Juanita responded, "None of your business." Unable to speak, but with a look of approval, Vincent just stared at Anthony. It is understandable that Vincent would react this way. Juanita was an incredibly beautiful and developed Mexican girl; but although their parents were from Mexico, Juanita and her older brother were both born in the United States.

In most cases, older brothers are generally very protective of their younger sisters. Miguel, however, not only liked Anthony a lot, he also owed him his life. A few months earlier, when Miguel was being attacked by a few of the upper-class, prejudiced kids in the neighborhood only because he was Mexican, Anthony intervened. Disgruntled by the fact that Mexicans were moving into their neighborhood, they were just about to kill Miguel when Anthony stumbled upon them. Grabbing the biggest attacker from behind, then holding a switchblade to his throat and directing it at all the other attackers, Anthony demanded, "Let him go, or this one dies."

Since Anthony had a reputation in the neighborhood of being crazy, the standoff did not last long. The attackers let Miguel go and ran off, though not without cursing and threatening Anthony. His courage not only got him instantly into the gang, it made Anthony an eternal friend of Miguel. And as a bonus, the event brought Anthony the liking of one of the prettiest girls in Brooklyn.

Because of having his innocence stolen from him not too long ago, it wasn't Anthony's intention to ever get involved with Juanita, or any other female for that matter. For argument's sake, let's say the incident with Miss Evans didn't happen and assume Anthony grew up with a normal appetite for female companionship. For a couple of reasons, if Anthony hadn't done what he did for Miguel, the odds of him being with Juanita, would be very slim. For one, there was the difference in race. When it came to relationships, it was a common belief even as late as the 1980s that people should stick with their own kind. And there was the age difference between Anthony and Juanita. Being two years older than the now-thirteen Anthony, Juanita looked more like she was eighteen. Standing at 5'4" and weighing about 110, Juanita had a chunky yet firm body. Having big brown eyes and full lips, Juanita wore her dark brown—almost black—pin-straight hair past her thin waist to her perfectly round, firm buttocks. But what attracted most men to her was that already Juanita possessed unusually large breasts. Already, at the age of just fifteen, Juanita wore a D-cup. Most men were willing to give their right arm to be with Juanita; Anthony, however, took a little more convincing. As it turned out—and proving how funny life is—if Anthony had not chosen to smoke the joint that day, he would probably never have engaged in that conversation with Juanita.

Keeping his promise to her, after returning the joint Anthony and Juanita returned to where they had been before. Breaking the ice and beginning the conversation, Anthony started by saying, "Juanita, I have to be honest. This was the first time I ever smoked pot." Knowing that it was indeed Anthony's first time, Juanita acted like she wasn't aware when she said, "Really? How do you feel?" Actually stoned, but needing to keep cool, Anthony answered, "A little weird. How am I supposed to feel?" Remembering her first time and relating to how he felt, Juanita, laughing, answered, "You're supposed to feel good and relaxed." Anthony—still able to use his wit even though high from smoking weed—responded, "Oh I'm relaxed. Otherwise there would be no way I'd be able to be here talking to you." Unconfidently, not knowing exactly what Anthony meant, Juanita inquired sadly, "Why not? Don't you like me?" Defending himself, and trying to explain his last statement in more detail, Anthony responded, "Na, that's not it at all. Maybe you didn't understand what I meant. Look, Juanita, I like you a lot. All I meant was that, because you are so beautiful, if I didn't smoke, I would be too nervous to talk to you." Satisfied with his answer and overwhelmingly happy inside, Juanita hugged Anthony, kissed him on the cheek and said, "Arhh, that's so sweet. Sorry for hugging you, but I am so happy you feel like I do."

Being a good-looking kid himself, Anthony's body was developed in a way that, just like Juanita's, made him look older. But because of his emotional problems, Anthony had a low self-esteem. This is one of the reasons why Anthony was skeptical when he said, "I'm really surprised, Juanita. You can be with anyone you want. Why do you like me?" Seeing something in Anthony that he couldn't see himself, Juanita asked, "Why not? What's wrong with you?" Very easy for him to provide the reasons, Anthony quickly explained, "Well for one, you're gorgeous, and I'm sure you can find a better-looking guy than me. Two, you're Spanish and I'm Italian. You don't have a problem with the difference in race? You're not afraid of what your friends and family might say? Then there is the age thing; you know you're like two years older than me. That isn't a problem?"

After hearing his concerns, Juanita became serious. Really wanting this to work, Juanita instructed him, "Okay, Anthony. I heard you out, now I want you to do the same. I want to tell you the whole truth, but promise me two things: One, you won't say nothing until I am finished. Two, look me in the eyes the whole time so you know I'm telling the truth." Becoming nervous from the anticipation, Anthony took a deep breath. Now, with a serious look on his face, and doing as she instructed, Anthony looked Juanita in the eyes and said, "Okay, I'm ready. Go ahead."

Having a secret crush on Anthony, and finally having the chance to let him know, Juanita took full advantage of the circumstances. Feeling that it was now or never, Juanita intended to tell Anthony everything she felt. There are so many people in the world who regret not taking the opportunity when it is put right in front of them. Juanita, determined not to be one of those people, changed her demeanor to serious—as Anthony did—and proceeded to explain. Returning the look into Anthony's eyes, Juanita began, "Let me start by saying I don't care what you are—Italian, Jewish, or whatever. I don't care how old you are, and I don't care what anyone thinks. You are gorgeous. If you don't believe me, just ask any girl in the neighborhood. They are all on your shit. Everybody says me and you would make a perfect couple. What it comes down to, I want you and nobody else." Flattered by what Juanita was saying, Anthony began turning red from embarrassment and attempted to turn away in disbelief. But before he was able to do so, Juanita—using the palm of her hand—grabbed Anthony underneath his chin and guided his face to where he could continue looking her in the eyes. Referring to his agreement to hear her out, caressing his cheeks gently with her fingernails, Juanita said, "Anthony, you promised."

Getting his attention once again, Juanita continued. "Remember a couple of months ago, when you brought Miguel to my house after he got jumped?" Confused, and realizing this was a question, Anthony didn't know how to respond. Nodding his head yes, and just about to say something, Juanita put her hand over Anthony's mouth and said, "Shhh, don't. Let me finish. I know you remember." Smiling, Anthony obeyed and continued looking Juanita in her eyes. Without prolonging it any further, Juanita continued to explain. "Well, I was looking out the window when you got there with Miguel. You were wearing that leather motorcycle jacket with only that white tank top underneath, and those ripped-up jeans. The second I saw you, I said to myself, Damn, he's hot." Rolling his eyes, not believing what Juanita was saying, Anthony said, "Bullshit!" Pretending to get angry, Juanita demonstrated a sourpuss on her face and said, "Anthony, let me finish." Still rolling his eyes in disbelief, but honoring her command, Anthony said, "I'm sorry, go ahead." Regaining her composure from before, Juanita continued. "Anyway. Like I was saying, I saw you on my porch talking to my brother, and without even knowing what happened—just the way you looked, with your long hair blowing in the wind—I knew right there I had to meet you. The minute you walked away, I ran downstairs and asked my brother who you were. I have to admit, I was a little disappointed when I found out you were Italian and only thirteen." With a puzzled look on his face, Anthony—breaking his promise—inquired, "Why? How old did I look? You thought I was Spanish?" Giving him a love tap on his arm, Juanita instructed him once again to "Stop interrupting." Realizing he had broken his vow, Anthony smiled and said apologetically, "Oops, sorry. Promise that was the last time." Accepting his apology, then holding his right hand in both of hers, Juanita began playing with Anthony's fingers and continued. "To answer your question: Yes, I admit when I saw you, I thought you were Puerto Rican. Because of your size, I thought you were like seventeen or eighteen. When I found out, I was kind of disappointed at first. But after Miguel told me what you did for him, I didn't care about nothing." Becoming truly serious now, holding Anthony's hand more firmly, Juanita looked him strongly in his eyes and said, "It's like I fell in love with you right there."

Not knowing how to respond to that display of affection, the only thing Anthony could think to say was, "Wow, I don't even know what love is." Not exactly what she wanted to hear at the moment, Juanita confidently replied, "Don't worry, you will." Inexperienced, Anthony then inquired briefly, "How so?" With a determined look on her face, Juanita replied, "I am gonna show you. I will do everything I know how until I get you to love me the same way I love you."

Being as it was the first time he ever had this type of conversation with a female, and being under the influence of the marijuana he had smoked, Anthony wasn't able to say what he wanted to at the moment. All of his responses seemed stupid to him. To avoid looking like a fool any longer, Anthony—attempting to change the subject—explained, "I'm sorry, Juanita. This was the first time I smoked weed, and I think I'm stoned." Waiting a long time to express herself and attempting to get back on the subject, Juanita replied, "I did something for the first time today too." Hoping that he wasn't the only one, Anthony asked curiously, "Oh yeah, what's that?" Hinting what she really wanted to follow up this conversation with, Juanita answered, "Even though it wasn't a real kiss, this was the first time I ever put my lips on a man's." Turning away in disbelief, Anthony said, "C'mon, get out of here. You can't tell me you never kissed anyone before?" Taking the statement offensively, Juanita stepped back and said, "Why not? What do you think of me?" Realizing how it sounded, Anthony—in an effort to try and retract his statement—explained, "Because, you're so beautiful you had to have boyfriends in the past that you kissed." To ensure Anthony she was telling the truth, Juanita—as she always would from that day forward—looked him in the eyes and said, "No way. Miguel would never let me have a boyfriend. Since my father died, my brother has been really protective of me." The explanation sounded reasonable to Anthony, but it also made him worry about himself. Wondering what Miguel would think, Anthony asked, "Why isn't he like that when it comes to me then?" Easily explaining the answer, Juanita responded, "Simple. Those kids would have killed him that day. You saved his life. Miguel was actually happy when I told him I wanted to be with you." Relaxed, and satisfied with all of Juanita's explanations, Anthony—jokingly and with a smirk on his face—asked, "Well, what took you so long to tell me you like me then?" Taking Anthony's question seriously, Juanita regretfully answered, "Because I was more nervous than you. Besides, every time we hang out, it's always with the others around. This was the only time we were almost alone. Then once I saw you smoke, I said to myself, here's my chance. That's why I snuck you that kiss." With his palms sweating, Anthony swallowed in a nervous reaction. Building up some courage, Anthony asked, "Juanita, did you like kissing me?" Feeling similar to how Anthony did at the moment, Juanita replied, "Yes, but I think it could be better."

It really wouldn't have mattered what Anthony said right at that moment. After just pouring out her heart, Juanita was going to do what she planned to regardless of Anthony's response. Juanita figured that if there was ever going to be anything between her and Anthony, he would automatically accept her next move. If for some reason Anthony rejected her, Juanita, however devastated, would have to accept her previous conversation as a loss and move on with her life. Determined, Juanita awaited Anthony's response to her last statement. Fortunately for both of them, to Juanita's statement that the kiss could have been better, Anthony inquired, "How?" As she so longed to do, Juanita—not a second after Anthony asked—put her arms around his neck. Pulling Anthony close enough to where he could feel her breast pressed against his body, Juanita closed her eyes, leaned up, and began kissing him very sensually. Inexperienced, yet doing what came naturally, Anthony put his arms around Juanita's waist and engaged their first kiss.

After carrying on the moment for about ten minutes,

Juanita and Anthony were interrupted by the others barging in from around the bend. The first one to say something was Joseph Jr. Pulling Anthony by the shirt out of Juanita's arms, Joseph jealously said, "C'mon, Anthony, we gotta go." Attempting to embarrass his little brother, and referring to him kissing Juanita, he proclaimed, "You don't know what you're doing anyway." Defending her newfound love, Juanita snapped back, "Oh, yes he does." Not yet satisfied with the time she had with Anthony, Juanita—watching her happiness being dragged off by his older brother—yelled, "Joey, please let me get five more minutes with him." As all men were, Joseph—being attracted to Juanita as well—flirtingly replied, "It depends what's in it for me."

Open-minded and willing to do anything for more time with Anthony, Juanita asked, "What do you want?" In bad taste, and referring to the kiss she just gave Anthony, Joseph Jr. responded, "What about the same thing you gave him?" Torn between desperately wanting to spend more time with Anthony and disgust at Joseph Jr.'s request, but not about to give in, Juanita used her wit and said, "No way, Joey. I'm sorry, but I love Anthony. The best thing I could do for you is set you up with my cousin. She's older, and she likes guys with blue eyes."

Beaten and aware of how he looked to everybody after his comment, Joseph Jr. surrendered to Juanita's request and said, "Alright, go ahead. Anthony, me and Vinny will meet you at the house." Also respecting the two new lovebirds' privacy, Tommy, leaving in the other direction, said, "Later, everybody. I'll see yous tomorrow." Not wanting to disturb his little sister and the kid who saved his life, Miguel also departed. On his way out, Miguel said, "Anthony, see you later. And by the way, welcome to the family." Embarrassed by her brother's comment Juanita replied, "Shut up, stupid," Still walking away, and changing the tone of his voice to serious, Miguel added, "Juanita, you too hurry home. It is Mother's Day, you know." With more important things on her mind, Juanita respectfully nodded her "yes" to her older brother then quickly directed her attention back to Anthony.

Not a moment after everyone had left, Juanita put her arms

back around Anthony's neck, looked him in the eyes, and said, "Alone at last, mi amore." The feeling mutual, Anthony replied, "Thank God." With himself leading this time, Anthony put his arms around Juanita's waist. Using his right hand, Anthony grabbed Juanita's buttocks and, as before, pulled Juanita's body close to his and began kissing her. Kissing repetitiously, and using their hands, Anthony and Juanita began to feel each other's bodies. Continuing in this fashion, Juanita—with a look of love in her eyes—said, "I am so happy I told you how I feel." Attempting to keep his cool, yet overwhelmed with excitement, Anthony responded, "Me too. I don't think we would ever be together if you didn't say something." Exactly what she wanted anyway, Juanita teasingly asked, "So what, you think we're together now?" Not realizing Juanita was joking, and feeling stupid for assuming, Anthony—stuttering as he spoke—replied, "Well, I thought—I mean, isn't this what? I was hoping that's what this meant." Before allowing him to finish, Juanita said softly, "Shhh, I know. I was just playing. Of course we're together." Becoming a little bit more serious, Juanita added, "And we are always gonna be together, forever."

After which, kissing him more strongly, Juanita began moving her hands down from Anthony's muscular chest. As Juanita's hands passed Anthony's chiseled stomach and made their way towards his groin, Anthony pulled away. Even though he enjoyed Juanita's advances, a flashback of the experience with Miss Evans entered his mind. Only attempting to please him, a confused Juanita asked, "What's wrong, baby? Did I do something wrong?" Avoiding the truth, yet realizing he had to explain his reaction, Anthony said, "Na, nothing's wrong. Everything is right. It's just that I'm getting—well, you know. And as much as I want to keep doing this, I really have to go." Satisfied by Anthony's answer, and at the same time disappointed by the timing, Juanita said, "I know, me too." After a slight pause, Juanita took a moment to think and added, "Hey, sweetie, I got an idea. First, give me one more kiss. Then we could exchange phone numbers, call each other tomorrow, meet somewhere, and continue where we left off today. Okay? Agreed?" Smiling,

Anthony took her in his arms once again and replied "Only on one condition, though — you walk me home."

After taking her kiss, Juanita smiled back and said, "I was going to walk you home anyway."

Just before the two began their short journey to Anthony's house, Juanita pulled out a pen from her pocket and, as discussed, exchanged phone numbers with Anthony. Referring to whether or not he wanted to go home, Juanita asked Anthony, "Ready?" Putting his hand in hers and beginning to walk in the direction of his house, Anthony replied, "Not really." As the two walked on, Anthony said, "You know something? I'm stoned and I have to go out to dinner tonight. I don't know how I am going to pull this off. You want to know something else? I will be thinking about you all night." Touched by Anthony's words, and at the same time attempting to advise him, Juanita responded, "Arrh, that's so sweet. Don't worry, baby, no one will notice you. By then it will wear off a little. Here's what you do — keep to yourself, try to eat a lot; that helps it wear off too. Then, before you know it, dinner will be over, you'll be home sleeping, tomorrow will come, and you'll be with me." Slightly relieved by Juanita's advice, Anthony took a deep breath and said, "Thanks, sweetheart, I hope so. I can't wait till tonight's over. I was so worried about getting pinned out. Besides, I can't wait to be in your arms again. I think I am going crazy tonight" As they continued to walk, Juanita — loving everything Anthony said — used her free hand to grab Anthony underneath his arm, and rested her head on his shoulder. Trying to prolong reaching their destination, Juanita replied, "Me neither, baby."

When they reached Anthony's block, Juanita suddenly lifted her head from Anthony's shoulder and let go of his hand. Looking around in despair, Anthony nervously asked Juanita, "What happened? What's the matter?" Becoming angry, Juanita jealously inquired, "Who's that girl in that window staring and smiling at you?" Not realizing to whom Juanita was referring, Anthony looked towards every window in their view with the exception of his own. Not seeing any girl looking towards them, Anthony asked, "Who? Where? What window?" Feeling betrayed by the boyfriend she had for about ten minutes, Juanita, now furious, demanded, "Don't act stupid, Anthony. She's right in front of us, staring and smiling right at you. Do I have to point? Just be honest, is that your girlfriend?" Truly dumbfounded and with no other alternative, Anthony looked towards his own house and discovered Josephina pointing and laughing out her window. Following which, Catholina and Maria had joined in. Now with all three nosy girls looking on, Anthony, turning bright red from embarrassment, turned back towards the still-furious. Calming her instantly, yet still uncomfortable himself, Anthony ensured her by saying, "Don't worry, sweetheart. This is my house. Those girls laughing and pointing, well, two of them are my sisters and the other is Vinny's sister. They are all getting ready to go out." At ease now and accepting Anthony's explanation, Juanita grabbed his hand again and replied, "I'm sorry. I'm very jealous when it comes to you. It's only 'cause I don't want to lose you to anyone else."

In the intoxicating frame of mind Anthony was in—torn between continuing this conversation and joining his family in the house—the only thing he could say was, "Don't worry, Juanita. You're never gonna lose me." Pausing a second, looking towards his house once again then back toward Juanita, Anthony added, "Except for today. Look, Juanita, there is nothing I want more than to be with you, but I really have to go." Understanding exactly how Anthony felt, Juanita replied, "I know. Me too. It's only one day. If you can, call me later." Not wanting to be teased by his sisters looking on, Anthony apologetically informed Juanita, "Look, I really want to kiss you goodbye, but they're looking and I don't want them to know my business. But yeah, if I can get home early enough, I will definitely call you."

Disregarding Anthony's dilemma, Juanita put her arms around his neck and gave him a long kiss on the lips. Saying so, but not really meaning it, Juanita said, "I'm sorry, I couldn't resist. You can call me anytime before nine." Not angry, yet slightly disturbed she didn't honor his request, Anthony—in an attempt to avoid offending Juanita—said, "Don't take this the wrong way. I love kissing you, but I'd just rather do it in private."

Developing a sad and confused look, an unconfident Juanita asked, "Why? Are you ashamed of me?"

Trying not to be misunderstood, and feeling he needed to explain in more detail, Anthony quickly responded, "No. Absolutely no. Okay, I said that wrong. I don't care about kissing you in public. I don't care if everyone knows we're together. I just don't want my sisters to see us kissing, because as soon as I go in now they're gonna be teasing and making fun of me." Relieved by Anthony's explanation, Juanita agreed and responded, "Okay, I understand now. I didn't know they were like that. So this means I could kiss you in front of anybody except your sisters. Right?" Taking a second to think about it, hesitating before he answered, Anthony replied, "Yeah." Looking up at their window, Anthony saw the girls still watching and giggling at him. Annoyed now, he turned back to Juanita and said, "See what I'm saying? I'm sorry, sweetheart, I'll try to call you later. If not, then I promise I'll call you tomorrow." Juanita agreed, smiled, then kissed the air in Anthony's direction. Beginning to walk home as she watched Anthony go into his house, Juanita said, "Bye, baby. I'll talk to you later."

Just as he expected they would, as soon as Anthony came into the house all three girls raced to hound him. Trying to be mature about her teasing, Catholina asked, "Who was that Anthony?"

Anthony was unable to answer because it was Josephina's turn to tease. She interjected, "Was that your girlfriend?"

Determined to avoid answering any of them, Anthony attempted to make his way to his room. As he reached the door to his room, Anthony—directing his remark at all the girls at once—demanded, "Why don't all of yous mind your business? I have to hurry up and get dressed." While Anthony walked away, Maria—of course having to put her two cents in and referring to Juanita's ethnic background—said, "She's a little hot tomale."

Thinking he had escaped, Anthony entered his room only to find Joseph and Vincent laughing at him as well. Not laughing because of the same reason as the girls were, and knowing that Anthony was stoned just like them, both of them began cracking up when they saw Anthony's facial expression as he entered the room. Observing them and accepting their humor, Anthony joined in by saying, "Woah, made it. Free at last," Continuing to laugh at him, Vincent replied, "Wow, that must have been hard." Still stoned and feeling estranged, Anthony replied, "You ain't lying. I feel like I am in a dream. Does smokin this shit supposed to make you feel this way?" Changing his demeanor from joking to serious, a concerned Joseph Jr. demanded, "Be quiet. You're gonna get us busted. The statement making him paranoid, Anthony nervously whispered, "What should I do? When does this wear off?" Angry from Anthony's inquiry, Joseph Jr. instructed, "Not till you go to sleep. Go take a shower and get ready for dinner. That will make you feel better." Taking his brother's advice, Anthony avoided any confrontation as he made his way to the bathroom to get ready for the Mother's Day dinner.

Later that night, the families as planned went out to dinner at a restaurant in the city called Beefsteak Charlie's. Traveling in Regina's 1971 Fleetwood Cadillac, both families were able to fit because of the size of the car. Automobiles back in those days were a lot larger than today, and Regina's Cadillac topped them all. The most difficult part of the evening for Anthony and Vincent was keeping their cool while sitting in the front between both of their parents. Both of them sweating by the time they reached the restaurant, Anthony and Vincent just sat there quietly during the whole the trip. Being well-off financially before the departure of her husband, Regina's car, along with her house, were already paid for. Although her husband had left her with no money, Regina was able to get back on her feet rather easily. Unlike Angela's situation when abandoned by Joseph Sr., Regina's children were old enough to stay home alone so that she could return to work. Even having limited work experience, or skills for that matter, Regina found work rather easily as a night driver for a local car service. Because her bills were rather minimal, Regina really didn't need to earn that much from any job she took. The driving job was perfect since it didn't pay a lot at all. Unlike Angela—not needing to pay rent and only having two kids to support—Regina was able to maintain her bills from what she made from her job. Getting accustomed to living without the extras they had when their father was in the picture would be the biggest challenge for Regina's family. It sounds fairly easy, but in truth it wasn't. Regina having only little control over them from the beginning, both of her kids began to rebel tremendously when she could no longer give them everything they wanted. That being the case, Regina's working at nights created a situation that was just asking for trouble.

Since Regina and Angela were both single parents, Mother's Day was always a special occasion for the families. It was the one and only day all the kids would be able to give back to the mothers who sacrificed so much for them. Although Beefsteak Charlie's wasn't the best restaurant in town, the gesture was deeply appreciated by the parents. The food was decent, but most important the restaurant was well within the kids' price range. Both of them already holding jobs as secretaries, Catholina and Maria picked up the majority of the bill. Josephina also chipped in with her babysitting money, and the boys with the money they accumulated from doing odd jobs around the neighborhood. The adults none the wiser to the boys' intoxicating condition, the main topic of discussion was Anthony's new girlfriend. Blaming their incoherence on the wine they had with dinner, Joseph and Vincent sat quietly while Anthony remained in the hot seat. Answering numerous questions from the girls, and listening to the back-and-forth opinions of the parents, he began to regret smoking pot on that day. Then, after thinking about it for a second, he realized that if he hadn't smoked, there would be a good chance he would never have known Juanita and gotten the chance to experience everything he had and everything he still would.

Isn't life funny that way? If one thinks about it, there has to be at least one time in everyone's life, that one specific choice he or she made changed the outcome of his or her life for years to follow. Whether the experience was good or bad, I'm sure everyone at one time or another used the phrase, "What did

I do to deserve this?" Was it fate that brought this on? Is there really a higher power that controlled what happened, or what will? Are we controllers of our own destiny? Or maybe it is a combination of both. Maybe our life choices are put there by a higher power, and it is up to the individual to choose which way to go. A matter of opinion; and depending what you want to believe, when you evaluate thoroughly you'll notice that there will always exist a choice you made that caused the outcome.

Anthony, however, didn't look at his life this way. Believing he didn't have a choice, he did whatever was expected of him. A true follower, he smoked weed that first day because he felt he had to. Being the in-control young lady Juanita was, even then, Anthony felt he had to get involved with her. Doing everything he did just to please others, Anthony would never do anything for himself. Filled with pain and suffering as he already was, by following this unhealthy pattern Anthony was looking at a long, miserable life.

As he promised, the moment he returned home from dinner Anthony called Juanita. Excited to hear from him, Juanita answered the phone, "Anthony. You made it." Because the high from the marijuana had worn off, Anthony—more himself now—replied, "Yeah, I know. Thank God. I almost didn't call." Disappointed, Juanita inquired, "Why not?" Being the respectful, considerate kid he was, Anthony responded, "Because it is almost nine. I don't want to disturb your mother or nothin'. I'm saying, it is Mother's Day." To display how important he was to her, Juanita informed him, "No. No way. I was sitting by the phone all night hoping you'd call. I was even gonna sleep by the phone, just in case you forgot and called later." Still respectful, Anthony responded, "Na, I wouldn't do that. Your mother would hate me." Speaking confidently, and assuring Anthony, Juanita replied, "No, she'd never hate you—not after what I told her about you. Matter of fact, my mother can't wait to meet the boy who saved her son's life and makes her daughter so happy." Embarrassed by Juanita's statement, Anthony, becoming uptight, asked, "What do you mean? What did you tell her about me? I can't believe you said something." Quickly attempting to calm Anthony down, Juanita complimented him and responded, "Why? What are you worried about? You're a great guy. Of course I am going to brag about you. Why? Aren't you gonna tell your mother about me?" Not having the same relationship with his mother as Juanita had with hers, Anthony explained, "Yeah, I'm gonna tell her about you. I can't say everything, but she's gonna know you're my girlfriend. Wait, I'm sorry. Are you my girlfriend?"

Without hesitation, leaving no doubt about it, Juanita answered, "Of course. Absolutely. And you better not forget it.

Even after talking on the phone for an hour, Anthony, being new at this, really wasn't sure how to talk to Juanita. Anthony's conversation, rather than sounding like a man talking to a woman, sounded more like a friend talking to another friend. On the other hand, Juanita was new at this as well. The difference was that, because of her beauty, Juanita always had guys try to sweet-talk her in the past. It wasn't that Anthony didn't want to talk to Juanita in the manner she was expecting, it was that he just didn't know how. Unaware of Anthony's inexperience, Juanita assumed he wasn't interested. Inadvertently working to his advantage, Juanita, her self-esteem lowered, would try that much harder to win Anthony's heart. As the night came to an end, Juanita's mother had to force her off the phone. The plan for the next day was that Anthony would meet Juanita on her corner in the morning and walk her to school. The two would then meet for lunch and walk home together after school.

When the following morning arrived, Anthony—groggy yet excited—hadn't been able to sleep through the whole night. Stirring up the nerves inside him all night, the anticipation of his date with Juanita would not allow Anthony to catch even one wink. Battling his siblings for use of the bathroom, he rushed to get ready for school. Way ahead of schedule, he planned to surprise Juanita by showing up at her house ahead of schedule. To his surprise, and spoiling his plan, as he opened his door the vision of an angel was standing before him. Wearing a black miniskirt and a tight-fitting V-neck, Juanita left Anthony speechless. Accustomed to seeing Juanita only in her street clothes, Anthony froze and could only stand with his eyes wide open and his mouth dropped to the ground.

"Well, you just gonna stand there?" Juanita asked. "Come give me a kiss." After honoring her request, Anthony, lost for words, asked, "What are you doing here? I thought we were going to meet on your corner."

As Anthony took her bookbag to carry it for her, Juanita answered, "I know. I couldn't sleep good. I couldn't wait to see you. Why? You're not happy to see me?" Still shocked by Juanita's appearance, Anthony answered, "Of course I am. It's just funny, because I was just about to go to your house and surprise you, and boom, here you are."

As the two began to walk, Juanita put her hand in Anthony's and her arm around his bicep, and said, "So, Anthony, do you like the way I look?" Attempting unsuccessfully to keep his eyes off Juanita's much-displayed cleavage, Anthony answered, "Yeah. I mean, wow. I mean, I am not used to seeing you like this." Smiling from his approval, referring to her breasts and noting that Anthony was ashamed for looking, Juanita assured him by saying, "It's okay, baby. You can look at them. They're yours, you know. I mean, this is why I dressed like this today—for you. You know I don't usually dress like this."

Nervous and not knowing how to respond, Anthony looked into her eyes and smiled. Smiling back, still referring to her breasts, Juanita added, "Yeah, you can look at them if you want. You can touch them, kiss them, whatever. And do you know why?" Swallowing nervously, Anthony curiously inquired, "Why?" Determined to please him and make him feel comfortable with her, Juanita—looking in Anthony's eyes—responded, "Well, for one, like I said they're yours. Two, I know you like me for other reasons; and three, my feelings for you are very strong. And Anthony, I want you to be the first one."

With his heart racing now, Anthony became speechless. Anthony felt the same as Juanita, but he didn't want to do to her what Miss Evans did to him. Still avoiding that experience, Anthony knew he had to say something to convince Juanita of his feelings for her. Arriving at the front of the school,

Anthony stopped walking and said, "Look, Juanita. You know I really like you. I like the idea of being your first and you being mine. The thing is, I want to be with you forever. I see others in relationships, and they rush things, then it ends. Now, I think I could really love you—soon. I just want to wait till that happens." Anthony's explanation making sense to her, Juanita sighed in relief. Juanita's heart touched by Anthony's words, she replied, "Wow, I'm happy you feel that way. Most guys can't wait to get into a girl's pants. To tell you the truth, I'm not sure I'm ready. I think—I mean, I know I love you. And I thought, if I gave myself to you, you would love me the same way."

Before giving Juanita back her books, Anthony kissed her on the lips and, while hugging her, said, "Don't worry, sweety, I will. If I'm gonna love any one, it will be you." Putting her head on his chest, Juanita replied, "Thank you. I can't wait." As the school bell rang to begin class, Juanita let Anthony go, kissed him again, and instructed, "Meet me here for lunch." Walking away backwards, Anthony smiled and nodded his head yes.

From then on through the remaining days of school, Anthony and Juanita would do everything the same way they did that first day. With all the good feelings that could be felt, there is nothing that could ever compare to the beginning of a relationship. Not only the getting-to-know-you part, but the physical aspects as well. Discovering each other for the first time, every day feels new. After all the walks to and from school, and all the lunches, Anthony had rapidly become addicted to Juanita's company. Because of his teasing sisters and jealous brother, Anthony usually spent the weekends at Juanita's house. Not having much money, they would spend most of their time in her house, and so Anthony became very close to Juanita's family. By the end of the school year, Juanita and Anthony were as close as any two people could be. Whenever you saw one, you would see the other.

The biggest day in the neighborhood—the day all the kids circled on their calendars, not a holiday but treated like one: the last day of school—had finally arrived. So important, more kids celebrated on this day more than any other during the whole year. To commemorate this significant event symbolizing the last day of structure and the beginning of a two-month bout of freedom, a party was thrown in a different person's house each year. Everyone in the neighborhood was invited, so not to attend would have been an insult. Even the kids who didn't attend school anymore celebrated. Vincent, one such kid, had dropped out of school shortly after his father left. Mainly street smart, Vincent had never succeeded in school anyway. Already having a major problem with authority by the first grade, Vincent was placed in a special school after throwing a chair in retaliation when his teacher called him stupid.

This year, since their mother was now working nights at the car service, it seemed logical for Maria and Vincent to have the party at their house. Vincent having few friends because of his wise mouth, and with Anthony spending most of his time with Juanita, the party was just what he needed. Throwing the party in his house this year would finally get the others to accept him. Maria not being the typically responsible older sister, in love with partying and chaos, not only did not object to the party—she assisted in putting it together. Both Anthony and Juanita attended these parties before, but it was special this year because they were attending it together. Since the party was at his best friend's house, it was only courteous that Anthony and Juanita assist in setting up the festivities. Anticipating her plans for Anthony, Juanita told her mother she was sleeping over at a friend's house.

After setting up the food and drinks, Maria called Vincent, who was in the basement with Anthony. Calling him with a sense of urgency, Maria yelled, "Vincent." Not normally respectful to his sister, yet feeling different today because she allowed the party, Vincent answered, "Yes, can I help you?"

Finding it strange how her brother answered, Maria instructed, "Me and Juanita are going to my room to get dressed. Can you and Anthony get the music ready?"

"No problem," Vincent said, feeling important now.

Sitting in front of the mirror in Maria's room dressed only

in her underwear while doing her make-up and hair, Juanita decided to confide in her.

Not knowing how to begin, Juanita nervously asked, "Maria. You know Anthony good, right?" Very proudly, Maria answered, "All my life he's been like my brother." Assuring her her plans were honorable, Juanita explained, "Well, I really love him. I am thinking about sleeping with him tonight for the first time. Since you know him well, how do you think he would think of me if I made the move on him?"

Touched by the confidence Juanita showed in her, Maria answered, "Ah, the first time. Well, knowing Anthony, you won't ever get it unless you make the first move. He's unusually respectful to women. Anthony won't try anything until he knows it is okay with you."

Confused now how to approach him, a worried Juanita asked, "Yeah, but what do I do to let him know? I really want him, but I don't want to say something slutty." Observing Juanita's body up and down, Maria—complimenting and assuring her, said, "You don't have to do much. Just get him alone. Use my room if you want. While you're kissing him, just take off your clothes and you won't have to say anything. If you do have to say something, just whisper in his ear. Say, 'Make love to me.'" Juanita curiously responded, "That's it? You think that will work?" From experience, Maria certain of her advice, answered, "If all that doesn't work, then Anthony is gay."

Just then—Maria and Juanita ready and heading down the stairs—the doorbell rang. Dressed similarly to the time Anthony walked her to school for the first time, Juanita asked him, "How do I look?" Looking at Juanita's black mini-skirt he loved so much, then at her revealing, white button-down blouse, a choked up Anthony answered, "Beautiful as usual." After giving him a kiss, Anthony and Juanita began greeting the entering guests together. As the night went on and the party progressed, the thirty to forty people in attendance—all smoking pot and drinking—began to get rowdy. Alcohol and drugs affect everybody differently. Some become violent, some calm. For some, though, the consumption of alcohol and drugs would make them do things they wouldn't if they were sober. These are the types of people who could make or break a party. The members of The Mutts were not troublemakers; they were made up of a group of kids who didn't have much but each other. However, if an outsider attempted to disrupt their tranquility in any way, the group would absolutely defend themselves. Now, not all of those attending the party were in the gang. Marc was one of these kids, though because of his crush on Juanita he always wanted in. But—not only for this reason but because there was nothing dysfunctional about his family and their finances were good—Marc would never be accepted. One of those people who become violent when intoxicated, Marc was allowed to hang around the gang only because of his connections in acquiring marijuana. The gang accepted as members only those who needed, not just wanted, a gang to belong to.

Marc, planning in advance for the evening, had brought some of his friends with him. Now—being drunk, jealous, and vindictive—Marc made his move. He had his friends lure Anthony away from Juanita with the promise of getting him on a baseball team. Anthony was by this ruse easily kept busy while Marc cornered Juanita. Once having Juanita out of sight, Marc—coming off friendly at first—asked, "How are you doin tonight?" In a very good mood because of her plans for her boyfriend, Juanita politely answered, "Good. I'm having a great time." Taking her friendliness as flirtatious, Marc quickly crossed the line. Juanita having the body that would tempt any man, an intocicated Marc, seeing how she was dressed, could not resist any longer.

Using his body to block Juanita from escaping, Marc said, "What are you with Anthony for?" Defending her man, and insulting Marc at the same time, Juanita responded, "Because he's the hottest guy here." Offended, but in an attempt to be witty, Marc retaliated, "How do you know if you never tried me?" Becoming irritated by Marc's advances, Juanita replied, "I don't want to try you. I'm happy with what I got." Not taking no for an answer, Marc put his hand on Juanita's chest and said, "You're gonna want me tonight."

Pushing Marc's arm away and yelling so that so everyone could hear her, Juanita said, "Get the fuck off of me."

Hearing the distressed voice of his girlfriend, Anthony, concerned, tried to come to Juanita's rescue and attempted to walk away from Marc's friends. Noticing that Marc's plan weren't working, one of his friends—in an attempt to help him—swung a beer bottle and broke it over Anthony's head as he was walking towards Juanita. Before they could do Anthony any more harm, the gang rushed over to aid him. Now the gang got involved, and nothing ends a party faster than when a fight breaks out, especially one that pours into the street such as this one did.

Unphased by getting struck in the head with a bottle, Anthony, with blood pouring from his eye, got up quickly and raced to Juanita's defense.

By her arms, Anthony grabbed Juanita—who had a terrified look in her face—and demanded, "What happened? Are you okay?" Concerned and upset by Anthony's injury, Juanita—hesitating yet answering anyway—responded, "While they had you over there, this motherfucker forced himself on me. He touched my tits and everything." Ignoring his own injury, Anthony angrily turned on Marc and demanded, "What the fuck, jerkoff? You know she's with me." Not taking Anthony seriously and having a feeling of superiority, Marc—getting very close to Anthony—replied, "So what? What the fuck are you gon—?"

But before Marc could finish his sentence, Anthony—like a pit bull attacking its prey—backslapped him across the face. Refusing him the chance to strike back, Anthony charged Marc and slammed him into the coffee table. Not holding back any longer whatsoever, Anthony pinned him to the ground with his knees and let rain a series of punches to his face.

Worried about the furniture, Vincent grabbed Anthony and said, "Okay, that's good. We'll take him outside from here."

But while Anthony was being held back, Marc—in an act of cowardice—sucker-punched Anthony in the mouth. Some members of The Mutts grabbed him and dragged him outside. Both Vincent and Juanita tried to calm him, but Anthony—determined to finish Marc off—broke free from Vincent's hold like a man possessed. Directing his anger at both Vincent and Juanita, he furiously demanded, "Get the fuck off of me." Anthony dashed outside after Marc, and Marc took an unsuccessful swing at his face. As Marc missed Anthony with his weak punch, Anthony followed up with a swivel kick, knocking Marc's feet from under him and causing him to crash to the ground. Now Anthony pinned his arms again, and this time he didn't stop punching him in the face until he was unconscious. Meanwhile Marc's friends were suffering beatings of their own from the rest of the gang.

Then—just as most fights and most parties end—the cops, called to the scene by one of the neighbors, stopped it. Not too concerned with the unsupervised party or the underage drinking, they merely sent everyone home. The only concern the cops had was who was responsible for leaving this kid a bloody pulp on the sidewalk. Of course, all the cop's questions would be in vain. No one attending that party would have ratted out Anthony. So after Marc came to, the cops took him home and left the situation alone. As far as the police were concerned, no felonies were being committed, and so there was no reason to bother themselves with the unnecessary paperwork.

After the party dispersed, Juanita cleaned up Anthony's face in the upstairs bathroom while Maria and Vincent cleaned up the house. Though disturbed in a way, Juanita—being the good girlfriend she was—calmly asked while cleaning up his wounds, "Are you alright?" Still a little hyped up and angry, Anthony replied, "Yeah. He got lucky with one punch, that's it." Answering proudly, yet with a sourpuss expression on her face, Juanita replied, "I know, I saw that. He only got you because we were holding you back." Then, after playing the fight over in his head and realizing the reason why she was different, Anthony remembered snapping at Juanita. He stopped her from cleaning his eye, took both of her hands in his, looked her in the eyes, and said, "Look Juanita, I am really sorry for yelling at you. It's just that I love you so much that after you told me what he did I lost it. All I could think about was killing that asshole." Speechless for a minute, not hearing anything else but one thing, Juanita asked, "What did you say?" Not sure what Juanita was referring to, Anthony repeated, "I was saying I was sorry for—"

Before Anthony could finish, Juanita stopped him and said, "Not that, the other thing."

Confused, Anthony thought about everything he just said and realized what Juanita wanted to hear again. A little shy, he built up the courage and replied, "Oh. You mean, 'I love you so much.'"

Just as he repeated it, Juanita gave Anthony a long, passionate kiss. She put her hands on both sides of Anthony's face, looked him in the eyes, and said, "I love you too, baby—so, so much." She followed this with a series of smaller kisses. Attempting to relax Anthony by rubbing his shoulders, Juanita—with tears of joys in her eyes—said, "Oh my God, I've been waiting so long for you to say that." With a regretful tone in his voice, Anthony—referring to the words Juanita was waiting to hear since she met him—replied, "I'm sorry it took so long, and I'm sorry for tonight." Nothing able to bother her now, Juanita joyously replied, "Don't be. So you just needed some time. As for tonight, I should not have held you back. After all, you got into that fight because of me." Anthony quickly interrupted. "No, not because of you. He started that shit, and I should not have taken my anger out on you." Attempting again to calm him down, Juanita continued to rub Anthony's shoulders and back, and then followed with a series of kisses to the back of his neck.

Trying to change the subject a little, Anthony replied, "C'mon baby, let's get out of this bathroom. Maybe we should help them downstairs." However, Maria and Vincent—not to Anthony's knowledge—were outside the bathroom eavesdropping on everything.

At the very moment Anthony and Juanita came out of the bathroom and attempted to go downstairs, Maria popped out and asked, "Where are yous going?"

"Downstairs to help you," Anthony said. Rooting for

Juanita to carry out her plan, Maria insisted, "No, no. Everything is taken care of. Besides, you just got cleaned up. You should really get out of that bloody shirt and go relax in my room."

Always accepting Maria as an older sister, and because he was still tense from the fight and really didn't want to help anyway, Anthony took her advice.

"You too, Juanita," Maria said. "Go to my room with him."

Following Anthony into the room, Juanita stealthily closed and locked the door. Anthony was attempting to loosen his neck by rotating his head. As she sat next to him on the bed, a concerned Juanita asked, "Are you okay?" Attempting to act cool, Anthony replied, "Just a little stiff from the fight, that's it, baby. I'm okay." Realizing her now-or-never chance, Juanita instructed Anthony, "C'mon, baby, lie on your front. I am going to give you the best massage."

Unaware of Juanita's real intention, and liking the idea, Anthony agreed. "Okay, but take it easy with me." After kissing Juanita, Anthony proceeded to do as she instructed. Turning around and laying on his stomach, Juanita—with more than a massage on her mind—put one leg over Anthony's body and sat in a squatted position on his buttocks. She started to dig her hands into Anthony's shoulders, then halted and said, "Wait, sweetheart, Maria's right. You need to take off this bloody shirt." Just as Anthony made his attempt to get up and remove his shirt, Juanita stopped him by saying, "No, baby, don't get up. I'll do it for you." After allowing Juanita to remove his shirt, and feeling the sensual manner in which she ran her hands up his back as she did so, Anthony began to realize Juanita's intention. Realizing his words would have been meaningless if he had done so after just proclaiming his love for her, Anthony did not want to hurt Juanita's feelings by denying her.

Lying on his stomach shirtless now, Anthony was right where Juanita wanted him. While continuing to rub Anthony's back sensually, Juanita decided to proceed with her plan. She indiscreetly unbuttoned and removed her own blouse. Still massaging Anthony's back, she removed her bra as well. Very close to accomplishing what she wanted, Juanita asked with her best sexy voice, "How does that feel?" Nervous because he knew what was about to happen, Anthony responded, "Oh, yeah, that feels great. Please, don't stop."

Juanita continued massaging. Then, unable to hold back any longer, she leaned forward and began to kiss the back of Anthony's neck. Still using her sexiest voice, Juanita asked, "And how does that feel?" Feeling Juanita's large, firm, and now bare breast on his back, and sure she was trying to seduce him, Anthony responded, "Wait, stop. Let me turn over." Letting him do so, and happy he did not reject her, Juanita—still in a squatted position—sat back down on Anthony's groin. It being her first time, Juanita was a little embarrassed to be topless in front of Anthony. With Anthony now on his back facing her, Juanita continued to kiss his neck and buried herself in his well-chiseled body while she caressed him with her hands.

After the incident with Miss Evans, Anthony never thought he would be able to enjoy sex with anyone. But becoming aroused, Anthony put his hands on Juanita's buttocks. Pulling her up so her face was level with his, Anthony asked, "Are you sure about this?"

Looking in his eyes, Juanita replied, "More than anything. I love you so much, I just want to make you happy." After kissing her again, Anthony responded, "I love you too. I couldn't do this if I didn't." Not knowing what Anthony meant by his last statement, but excited by it anyway, Juanita buried his face in her breast and, using a louder voice than before, said, "Oh, Anthony, make love to me. Make love to me now." As he awkwardly removed his pants and underwear, Anthony—feeling her breast and kissing her neck—asked, "Are you ready?" Overly excited herself, Juanita responded, "Oh, yes, I'm ready."

As she removed her skirt and panties, Juanita felt for Anthony's penis. Once his fully-erect penis was in her hand, Juanita, becoming frightened, replied, "Oh my God, it's so huge." Worried by this, Anthony asked, "Is it okay? Do you like it?" Feeling Anthony's size in her hand, and feeling him getting softer after her reaction, Juanita began stroking him and said, "I didn't mean to react like that. Yeah, I love it. It's great. I wasn't expecting it to be this big. Anthony, put it in, slowly."

At first because of her tightness, Anthony's whole penis could not fit inside of her. But as he entered, he watched Juanita's facial expression turn from pain to pleasure. Still extremely tight, Juanita moved her body up and down on top of Anthony. Since it was their first time together, both Juanita and Anthony were very clumsy during their moment. After switching positions a few times, it wasn't until a couple of hours before Anthony and Juanita were comfortable. But once she adjusted to Anthony's size and the initial pain was gone, Juanita became more active. With Anthony now on top, Juanita—acting strictly on impulse—forced him onto his back in their original position. Able to take him all in now, Juanita climbed atop Anthony. With her hands on his chest and Anthony's penis throbbing inside of her, Juanita rotated herself harder and faster. As Anthony ran his hands to and from her breast to her buttocks, Juanita's moans became louder and less spaced. Hearing Juanita's screams and watching her expressions, Anthony became overwhelmed with excitement. Just when he could no longer hold back and he had reached his climax, Juanita's fingernails dug deep in his chest, Anthony heard one last loud scream. Just as he let go, he felt a warm, wet, familiar sensation on his penis and legs.

While both Juanita and Anthony wound down their heavy breathing, Anthony took one last deep breath of delight and gave Juanita a long satisfying look. Noticing her nail marks in his chest, Juanita rubbed them softly and said, "Oh my God, I'm so sorry." Pulling Juanita's body down towards his, bringing her head just below his chin, Anthony replied, "Na, don't worry about it." Still inside her, yet only semi-erect now, an unconfident Anthony inquired, "How was it? Caressing his body and kissing his chest, Juanita responded, "That—that was amazing." Curious about his performance, and trying to gather as much information as possible, Anthony asked more specifically, "I'm saying, though, Juanita, was it everything you thought it would be? Did I do everything right?" Lifting her head to talk to Anthony face-to-face, Juanita replied, "Well, there is just one thing." Discouraged and worried, a disappointed Anthony asked, "What? What did I do wrong?" Seeing his anguish, and not wanting him to take it the wrong way, Juanita quickly explained, "No, nothing. The sex was perfect. It's just that—well, Anthony, you came in me." Observing Juanita's tense expression, Anthony replied, "I know. I'm sorry. I couldn't help it; you were on top of me, and I couldn't speak." Observing Anthony's sincere guilt, which was not her intention to cause, Juanita—trying to boost his confidence—said, "Don't get me wrong. I mean I loved it. It's just tha—what happens if I get pregnant?" To ensure his loyalty, Anthony—quickly consoling Juanita's worries—replied, "Look, Juanita, I'm not trying to get you pregnant. We're both too young for that. But if it happened by accident, I would stick by you no matter what. I'm not going anywhere. But you're right. The next time we do this, I will be more careful." Satisfied and believing Anthony, making her way up his body to kiss his lips, Juanita responded sensually, "Well, we'll see, because the next time is right now." Anthon again erect inside of Juanita, the two went for the second time. As promised, Anthony was indeed more careful this time.

Not having the same enjoyment when Anthony pulled out at the end, and to keep him from having to do so, Juanita decided she would begin taking birth control pills.

After breaking the ice that first time, Anthony and Juanita could not stop having sex from then on. Some days they had sex three or four times; and each time it became better than the last. For Anthony and Juanita, sex with each other became an addiction. Never again did they ever have to wonder what to do when they were bored. Even when the two young lovers did have other plans, they would blow them off just to have sex. Quickly becoming their favorite thing to do, once Anthony and Juanita became more familiar with each other the sex became more frequent. Anthony and Juanita were each other's first for everything. The first time the two tried oral sex, it was with each other. The first time they tried anal sex, it was with each other. The first time they tried any kind of sex, it was with each other. Their sex life was so healthy that it became sickening to others. It wasn't only because their relationship was new; Anthony and Juanita kept this trend on for the next five years they were together. But it wasn't only their sex life that made their relationship so strong. Their doing things together for the first time did not apply only in the bedroom. The first time they smoked weed was with each other. Their first date was with each other. The first time they learned to drive and ride motorcycles, they learned together. If there ever existed a perfect relationship in the history of mankind, it would probably have been this one.

Arguments will happen in any relationship, and in Anthony and Juanita's case their arguments were usually about the same thing. Quite frequently, since both were attractive, someone would try to pick one of them up. Thinking about losing the love of your life could be a very scary feeling. Not certain if it is more frightening for a man or a women, when faced with the dilemma everyone reacts differently. In general, when a woman is jealous, she'll get more sad than angry. If there is a fight to pick, she'll usually pick it with her man. When a man gets jealous, he'll get very angry and territorial. The fight the man picks is always with the other man. In Anthony and Juanita's relationship, both reacted exactly the same way when jealous. It was no secret in the neighborhood that Anthony and Juanita were dating, and considering Anthony's reputation as a fighter, the guys in the neighborhood generally left Juanita alone. But the same rule did not apply for the girls in the neighborhood when it came to Anthony. Neither did it apply to guys from other neighborhoods when it came to Juanita. Needless to say, there would be many instances when both would have to defend the other's honor after they had been approached. On the one hand, Juanita couldn't help but to receive a lot of male attention. Even when she was walking hand-in-hand with Anthony, no man could resist looking at her. The looking, however, didn't bother Anthony as much as when they felt the need to say something. This in turn would give Anthony no choice but to get into a lot of physical conflicts. It is not certain whether or not Juanita enjoyed Anthony always fighting for her. Many females love to see their man act this way. Juanita, though, always acted as though his fighting were a problem. But since he won all the time, Juanita let it go rather easily.

On the other hand, when a female would do the same with Anthony, Juanita wasn't so lenient. Yes, she got into her share of scuffles, but for her part Juanita would blame Anthony for looking so good. Seemingly ridiculous—yet true because of his overall appearance, his toughness, and his altogether pleasant attitude—Juanita became angry with Anthony for attracting so many females. Once he began to make money selling drugs, her jealousy became that much more horrendous, and she would not allow him to go anywhere with out her.

When Juanita wasn't angry, she was very good to Anthony. Anything Anthony wanted, Juanita would do. He was welcomed into her home not as a boyfriend but as a husband. Juanita's mother loved Anthony, and she loved having him there to make her daughter happy. As all young lovers do, Anthony and Juanita talked constantly about marriage. Raising a family, buying a house far away, and living the American dream were what Anthony and Juanita wanted.

It would be nice to say that everything worked out for Anthony and Juanita. It would be great to tell you that this match made in heaven accomplished all their dreams. It would also be great to end this tale with the two living happily ever after. But this story is about real life, in which the choices you make make you the person you are. However, as many know, sometimes life is fair, but most of the time it is not.

Of course, one can't always predict the consequences of one's choices. The choices in this story are not ones that were carefully thought out. The choices in this story are the ones that are made at an impulse, or in the heat of the moment. They are the choices we wish later in life that we could take back.

When Anthony spoke to me about Juanita, it was obvious he was still carrying a lot of guilt inside. It was clear to me that he felt responsible for what happened. Anthony had made choices he wished he hadn't. After hearing the turn of events, it is understandable why Anthony would feel this way. Even though Anthony wasn't directly responsible for what happened, the result may or may not have been different, whether or not his choices had been.

Anthony never told Juanita about his experience with Miss Evans. Neither he nor Juanita had been mature enough to speak about this subject. But some will also believe, no matter what the ages involved, that if two people loved each other as much as Anthony and Juanita did, they should be able to talk about anything. Today, Anthony can not even justify why he kept this a secret from her, or any one else for that matter. Although sensible to him at the time, Anthony—knowing what he knows now—wishes that he told Juanita everything.

One reason Anthony held back was because of how Juanita perceived Anthony to be. Believing throughout their five-year relationship that nothing could ever hurt him, Juanita thought Anthony was indestructible and had no weaknesses. Looking back at it now—especially since Anthony was only a defenseless little kid at the time of the molestation—it is silly to believe that Juanita would think less of him if he had told her. Because the experience is what made Anthony the tough kid he was, surely Juanita wouldn't blame him for losing that fight. Especially since then, Anthony never lost another fight again.

Yet there was another reason Anthony kept the rape secret—Juanita's jealousy. When getting to know her, especially as a teenager, being molested could be a very difficult experience to have told her about. Dropping a bomb like that could be the difference in whether or not someone wants to be with another. It was Juanita's belief that she was Anthony's first, as he was hers. Since the two began having sex very early in their relationship, it became too late for Anthony to tell Juanita everything there was to know about him. As time went on, Anthony noticed that being each other's first had been very important to Juanita. With that in mind, and Juanita's jealous nature being a factor, Anthony—even though forced—decided never to let her know there was another before her. Anthony would regret this choice later.

One night, as Vincent and Maria were getting dressed to

go out, Anthony and Juanita were laying together after just having made love. Anthony lay on his back, and Juanita cuddled up beside him with her head resting on his chest and her arm draped over his waist.

"Do you want to go out with them tonight?" Anthony asked.

Although she loved going out dancing with him, Juanita did not want her good mood spoiled by all the attention Anthony would inevitably receive from other women. After thinking about it a moment, Juanita replied, "Not tonight. I don't feel like fighting off all those bitches that are on your shit."

Giggling while doing so, Anthony responded, "Please, Juanita. You think too much of me." Noticing Anthony wasn't taking her seriously, Juanita lovingly patted Anthony a couple of times on his stomach, then said, "Oh, really? You think that's funny? You think I'm joking?" Using his wit, and without hesitation, Anthony replied, "Matter of fact, yeah. You have more guys sweating you than I have girls sweating me. I'm the one who has to worry." Flattered by Anthony's statement, then ensuring her devotion, Juanita responded, "Worry. Worry about what? I know what I have. I ain't going nowhere."

Attempting to put Juanita on the spot, and curious how she'd answer, Anthony inquired, "Oh yeah? What do you have?" Seeming to already knew ahead of time what she was going to say if Anthony ever asked this question, Juanita was more than prepared when she elaborated, " I have a man with a giant heart. I have a man that would do anything for me. He is not only intelligent but street-smart too. I have a man with the perfect face, beautiful hair, and an incredible body. Oh yeah, one more thing. I have a man who was blessed with an enormous cock." Astonished by Juanita's readiness and lost for words, all Anthony could think of saying was, "Wow. I guess you know what you have." Continuing to make Anthony feel good, Juanita added, "I couldn't live if I lost you to someone else. This is why I try to be good to you. This is why I try to keep you only to myself. And this is why I don't like going out."

Understanding her completely now, Anthony said, "I feel

the same way you do, baby. That's why I do everything you want. That's why I give you anything you want. It doesn't matter who tries to get with me; I am yours forever and you'll never lose me. I only ask if you want to go out because I don't want you to get bored with me. I love you so much, baby." With her heart pounding in delight, a satisfied Juanita responded, "Ahrr, I love you too, baby—so, so, so much. Look, I am not saying this because I agree with you. As long as we're together, I'll never get bored with you. But if you want to go out tonight, Let's go."

Thinking about it a moment, Anthony paused, then answered, "Na, I don't. But I don't want Vincent and Maria to think we only come here to use their house. What do you think? Why? What do you want to do?" Without saying the words, Juanita moved her hand slowly from Anthony's chest, over his stomach, and down to his groin.

Getting Anthony's attention by massaging his testicles and semi-erect penis, Juanita said, "Oh, I could think of a couple of things to do." Torn between the temptation of Juanita's advances and disappointing his lifelong friends, Anthony replied, "Woah, decisions, decisions, decisions. Hmm, I know. Let's do this. We'll go out for a little while only, just until Vincent and Maria hook up. Then we'll come back here and finish where we left off. This way I don't feel like I am using them just for their house." Not angry, but a little disappointed, Juanita agreed, replying, "Ahrrr, baby, but I'm so comfortable right where I am right now. You're right, we do kind of owe it them." Attempting to prolong getting out of bed, Juanita gave Anthony a series of kisses from his stomach all the way up to his chest.

Afterwards, rolling on her back, Juanita stretched, let out a loud sigh of pleasure, then yelled aloud, "Maria. Wait for us, we're going out with yous." Excited, Maria burst into the room and asked, "Really? Yous are comin' out? No kiddin'?" Startled by Maria's entrance, Anthony quickly tried to cover up the naked lower half of his body. He was barely successful in his attempt, and Maria—catching a good look at Anthony's package—said jokingly, "C'mon, what are you worried about? I seen it before, don't forget who used to change your diaper when you were a baby." Joking along, Juanita proudly replied, "Well, it's a lot different now." As Anthony turned red from embarrassment, Maria—keeping the awkward moment going—responded, "Yeah, I see that. Now I know why Juanita always wants to stay in all the time." Agreeing without saying a word, Juanita, a proud look on her face, just nodded her head yes. After a slight pause, Maria, dancing in place, added, "Not tonight, though. Tonight we're gonna parrrty. C'mon, Juanita, let's get ready."

They went to L'amores. They enjoyed the buzz from the alcohol and marijuana while the other members of the gang joined them.

Maria turned to Juanita, who was nestled next to Anthony, and said, "Come with me on the dance floor. I need a man tonight too."

Not wanting to, Juanita looked to Anthony for help. But before he could say anything, Maria took Juanita by the arm and insisted, "C'mon Juanita. He'll be right here waiting for you when you get back."

"Go ahead," Anthony said. "Don't worry."

Just then, not two seconds after they had reached the dance floor—exactly what Juanita feared would happen if she left him by himself—Anthony was approached by two girls who had been watching him since he walked into the club. With short, bleach-blond hair and blue eyes, both girls looked like they could be twins wearing their best, sluttiest matching outfits. Observing the girls making their way towards him, Anthony—to avoid friction between them and his overly jealous girlfriend—tried to walk away, but before he could make his escape the two girls— who to Anthony were two Miss Evanses—cornered him.

The first, getting very close to Anthony's face (due to the loud music), introduced herself and her friend as Lisa and Diane.

To avoid being rude, but looking away, Anthony said, "Nice to meet you."

"Well, aren't you gonna tell us who you are?" the persistent Diane asked.

"I'm Anthony, and this is my best friend Vincent coming this way now."

Not interested in Vincent, the snobbish Lisa said, "We came over to meet you, not him."

"Yeah," Diane said. "We want you, not him." Flattered, yet avoiding leading them on, Anthony replied, "I'm sorry, then. It's too bad—see, I'm with somebody. Vincent here, though, isn't. He's really cool and single."

By this time, Juanita and Maria, in company with Miguel, approached Anthony and the two blondes.

Maria, having faith in Anthony, said to Juanita, "Just watch. Anthony is gonna diss them." Unsure of Maria's statement, a worried Juanita replied, "What? Are you crazy? They're gonna steal him from me." Certain that Anthony would do what she expected, Maria quickly responded, "No way. Wanna bet? I seen him do this before, and you should too."

Lisa, still intent on the menage, said, "I'm sure Vincent is nice and everything, but that is not what we're looking for tonight. Right Diane?"

Agreeing with Lisa and elaborating, Diane added, "Yeah, that's right. We're looking for a hot guy like you. Someone we can both do tonight."

With bad flashbacks of his molestation, Anthony said, "Well, yous two are looking in the wrong place. I'm sure yous will find someone to take yous up on that offer, but like I said before, I'm with someone. I love her and I sure the hell ain't giving her up for you two skanks."

Turning to Diane in disbelief, then turning back towards Anthony, Lisa replied, "Skanks—yeah, that's right. So what? But you're a retard if you don't jump on this chance."

"I'm a retard? Why? Cause I love my girl? Cause I don't want a disease? Cause I don't want my cock to fall off? Get the fuck outta here; I'd be a retard if I went with you," Anthony said confidently.

"So you'd rather be with that nasty spic girlfriend you were with than us?" Diane said. "Yeah, right. Good luck keeping your cock with that one." Furious from that last statement, losing control and talking loud for everyone to hear, Anthony replied, "What? What'd you say? You fucking white trash bitches, you seen me happy with my girl and tried to pick me up anyway. Then you have the nerve to call her nasty. Get the fuck out of my face before I spit on both of you." Testing him, and trying to get him to bite, the girls got up in Anthony's face and said provokingly, "Go ahead, do it. I dare you, spic lover."

Now Vincent intervened, pulling Anthony away, and Maria held Juanita back as she began screaming at Lisa and Diane.

"What's up now? Call me a spic to my face. Come on, you want to fuck with my man, then you gonna have to fuck with me."

Now the bouncers arrived and insisted the gang leave. Diane and Lisa, seeing they were overmatched, quickly walked away.

Once outside, Anthony and Juanita, still fuming, took their anger out on each other. First Anthony—not liking the fact Juanita just sat back eavesdropping, yelling aloud—inquired, "What were you doing behind me? Why didn't you step in sooner? What were you waiting for? What? Did you want to see if I was gonna go with them?"

In an effort to keep Maria out of it, Juanita said, "What the fuck you yelling at me for? This is why I didn't want to come here in the first place. It never fails—the minute I walk away from you, some bitches swarm around you like flies on shit." Referring to the conversation they had earlier in the day, Anthony answered, "So, I told you how I feel. I told you I'm not going anywhere. What? You didn't believe me? You don't trust me? You had to let me get in it with those twats to prove it to you? So what now? You happy? You satisfied?" Still not letting Anthony know it was Maria's idea, yet answering honestly, Juanita snapped back, "Yeah, matter of fact I am. Maybe that's what I needed. Cause a person could say something all they want, but you never really know they're telling the truth until you see it with your own eyes."

It wasn't often that Anthony cried, but seeing that tear fall from his eye for the first time touched Juanita dramatically.

Then—after hearing Anthony's sad voice say, "I can't believe this; after all we've been through, you still don't trust me"—Juanita froze. Not sure how to react, Juanita was about to surrender and hug Anthony apologetically. Then Anthony proclaimed, "Na, fuck this. When you're ready to trust me, I'll be at Vincent's." Then in an instant, leaving Juanita in her own guilt, Anthony ran off..

Feeling the guilt of her immaturity, Juanita broke down crying and looked for comfort in her brother's arms. Not knowing what to think, Juanita desperately inquired, "I lost him, didn't I, Miguel? The best man in the world, and I let him go." In an effort to console and reassure his little sister, Miguel responded, "No, no, baby girl. He's just angry right now. By tomorrow, he'll cool off and everything will be back to normal." Disagreeing and unconfident, Juanita replied, "No, not this time. This time it's over. I never hurt him like this before, and he never walked away from me during a fight before either." Continuing to give brotherly advice, Miguel explained, "Look Juanita, I know what you were trying to do, but put yourself in his shoes. I'm saying, that was a pretty stupid thing to do. How would you feel if Anthony showed that he didn't trust you?" In agreement, Juanita answered, "I know. I was stupid. It wasn't even my idea, it was Maria's." Shaking his head in disapproval, Miguel added, "Still you went along with it. I'm saying, What were you thinking?" Explaining her reasoning Juanita replied, "I just wanted proof of his love, his loyalty, his devotion. It seemed like a good idea at the time. I never thought it would escalate like that. It was a simple, innocent, stupid, stupid, stupid plan."

Disagreeing with her reasoning, Miguel became angry, then preached, "Proof of his love? Are you kiddin? You can't tell how much that kid loves you? Shit, if you had any doubt, you could've just asked me—or matter of fact, any one in the neighborhood. Look, Juanita, I'm your brother. I am always on your side, and I'll always tell you the truth. And the truth is, there are mad bitches on Anthony's shit. He could have any one he wants, but you know something? He don't care. He never pays those bitches no mind, because all that kid wants is you. You should be able to see this already. Really, Juanita, look at everything he does for you. Like I said, baby girl, I am your brother, and I am always on your side. But Juanita, I wouldn't be a good brother if I didn't tell you this. This time Juanita, you were wrong."

Her eyes watering from sadness, Juanita—realizing her mistake—pleaded, "Okay, I know I was wrong. I don't need any more lectures. What I need is your advice how to get him back. What do I do now?" Determined to help his sister and cheer her up at the same time, Miguel replied, "Look, just relax. Let Anthony cool off tonight. I'm sure he doesn't want to lose you either. First thing tomorrow, you go see him and tell him how sorry you are. Once he forgives you—and he will forgive you—give him the best blowjob of his life."

Though that was exactly her plan, Juanita was still surprised her brother say it, and she stood there with her mouth open in shock.

"That's right," Miguel said. "Don't stand there in shock like you never did it before. You owe it to him. You open that big mouth of yours as wide as you can, and you suck his dick better than you ever did before. Then, when you're finished, it wouldn't hurt if you sucked it again." Smacking Miguel's arm playfully, then giving him a hug, Juanita said, "Thank you, Miguel. I feel a whole lot better. You truly are a great big brother."

Meanwhile, as Juanita was being schooled by her older brother, a similar conversation was taking place between Anthony, Vincent, and Maria.

"How'd you get here so fast?" Vincent said—amazed that Anthony was already sitting on the porch when he and Maria arrived in a cab. With no enthusiasm whatsoever, Anthony answered, "I ran." Surprised by Anthony's answer, needing to hear it again, Vincent questioned, "What? What do you mean you ran?" Elaborating in more detail for Vincent, Anthony responded, "Yeah, I was drunk, and Juanita pissed me off so much I got jumpy. So instead of doing something stupid, I just ran away from her." Concerned for Juanita's safety, Maria—joining in the conversation—interrupted angrily, "So you just left her there by herself and ran away?" Quickly becoming defensive,

Anthony snapped back, "Na, I didn't leave her alone. She had her brother there. I just couldn't look at her after what she did." Believing Anthony's reason to be petty, Maria asked, "What'd she do that was so bad? To see how much you love her?"

"Why don't you stay out of it?" Vincent asked Maria. "This is between him and her."

"It's alright, Vin. Maria needs to understand it is not okay to spy on someone—especially after all the time we been together and she still don't trust me." Before Maria could reply, Vincent interrupted. "Look, both of yous, it is four in da morning. Yous wanna argue about this, why don't yous do it inside da house?" Both agreeing, Anthony and Maria followed Vincent inside their house.

After turning on the lights and the television, all three of them sat down in the living room as Vincent proceeded to roll a joint. Trying to keep the conversation from escalating into a loud Italian shouting match, Maria—pleading her case—calmly explained, "Anthony, you know I love you like my brother, and I want the best for you. And the truth is, Juanita really is the best girl for you. She's smart, she's loyal, she's gorgeous, and she is so madly in love with you. She'll do anything that you want her to Yous are perfect for each other. I'd hate to see you give her up and end up with someone that makes you miserable—like for example, those two bitches who caused all of this." Smoking the joint that Vincent just rolled, Anthony felt the need to be honest about how he felt. After taking a couple of pulls from the joint, Anthony—passing it on—elaborated, "There's no doubt in my mind that Juanita is the perfect girl for me. It don't even matter that she's so jealous. Shit, I am just as bad as she is, if not more. The thing is, I never slept around, I never kissed anyone else. Shit, I don't even check out other women like normal guys do. Not only am I always with her, when I am she sees me happy having her around all the time. So my point is, I never gave her any reason not to trust me. So when she spied on me tonight, it really hurt. I know, too, when a woman doesn't trust her man, eventually she is gonna go with someone else. If the woman thinks her man is cheating, she also will cheat. Maria, I just couldn't deal with that."

After listening to Anthony's concerns, Maria realized his reasoning wasn't so stupid and immature after all. As were the tears he had been trying to hold back, the pain shown in Anthony's eyes was genuine. Having a legitimate excuse for what he did, it was understandable that Anthony was trying to prevent himself from getting hurt. However, Maria knew something Anthony didn't. Something that would not only ease Anthony's mind but clear up this whole misunderstanding. Determined to make the peace between Anthony and Juanita, Maria explained, "Look Anthony, this is all just a big mistake. I've hung with Juanita; and take my word for it, she'll never go with another man. That girl is so whipped it ain't funny. You got her so bad, it's actually sad. Juanita won't even let another guy talk to her. We had to leave the dance floor because of all the guys trying to talk to her."

"Really?" Anthony inquired.

"Yeah, she told me that she just wanted to go back near you. And she wasn't spying on you. Maybe that is what you thought, maybe that is what it looked like, but I made her do that." Confused by Maria's explanation, Anthony curiously asked, "What do you mean, you made her do that? You're telling me you made Juanita spy on me? Get da fuck outta here." Continuing her attempt to convince Anthony, Maria added, "Na, Anthony, hear me out. The minute she saw those girls talkin to you, she was gonna step to them"

Quickly, a curious Anthony asked, "Then why didn't she?" Answering quickly herself, Maria said, "Because I know you. I knew you were going to diss them. So I told her to wait back and watch. So it wasn't that she didn't trust you—Juanita just wanted to see you treat those girls like shit."

Shaking his head no, not sure what to think, Anthony replied, "I don't know, Maria. It still doesn't make sense. That's not Juanita. She never did that before." Resting her case, Maria quickly insisted, "That's right, she never did that before. So what does that tell you?" Feeling ashamed of his reaction now,

Anthony responded, "It tells me I should tell her sorry. Maybe I did look at it wrong. I just wish Juanita told me what she was up to. She knows how stupid I am. But you're right, she's a real good girl. I would be even more stupid if I let her go." Feeling good about her contribution, Maria replied, "Yeah, she is a great girl. And you know me, I don't usually say that about people that aren't Italian."

Swallowing his pride, Anthony said, "Thanks, Maria. First thing tomorrow, I'll call her and tell her I'm sorry." Unsatisfied by Anthony's plan, Maria asked, "Tomorrow? Why tomorrow? Why not call her right now? That's what I hate about yous men—even when you are wrong, you always want to wait. Let me give you some more advice: Women want men to go after them right away." Respectfully, Anthony answered, "What are you—nuts? It's too late. I'll wake up her mother. Besides, she probably hates me right now anyway." Contradicting Anthony's belief, Maria responded, "What—are you nuts? Juanita's probably waiting by the phone for you to call right now. I bet she's dying for that make-up sex. Anthony, since it was my idea, I kinda feel responsible for yous fighting. I'd feel a whole lot better if I knew everything was alright with yous." Still not sure what to do, Anthony hesitated, then said, "I don't know." Determined to obtain her peace of mind, Maria insisted, "Look Anthony, I'll call the house. If Juanita answers, I'll give you the phone; if her mother answers, I'll take the blame for callin so late."

Just then, back at L'amores, Juanita and Miguel were awaiting a cab.

"I can't wait till tomorrow," Juanita said. "I need Anthony right now. Do you think he's still mad?" Answering totally honestly and confidently, Miguel responded, "Yeah, probably. Maybe not like before, but still mad. Don't worry about it—by tomorrow, Anthony will be waiting for you with open arms." With her feeling of guilt overwhelming, Juanita—thinking the worst—inquired, "Yeah, but what happens he meets someone tonight? And because he's mad, he goes home with her and forgets all about me. Miguel, I'll die if that happened." Assuring

Juanita of Anthony's loyalty, Miguel replied, "No way. You're crazy, baby girl. That boy ain't like that. He loves you to death, and you better stop thinking like that about him. That's why he thinks you don't trust him. Anthony's probably doin' the same thing you are. I bet he's at Vincent's house being calmed down and advised by both Vincent and Maria. But if you're really that worried, call him at Vince's and see what's up."

Liking the idea brought up by her older brother, yet hesitant to do so, Juanita—after a moment of thinking about it—

couldn't resist. Without wasting another second, her heart racing and her anxiety skyrocketing, Juanita jumped up from her squatted position and replied, "Alright. I am gonna do it. I'm gonna call him. I won't be able to sleep if I don't. I have to know for sure. Besides, since you said that, honestly, I can't get his giant cock off my mind. I'll truly go crazy if he stuck that shit in someone else. Do me a favor, Miguel, wait here for the cab." Silently and without argument, Miguel just motioned with his hand for his sister to go.

At the house, just as Maria was about to call Juanita, the phone rang, startling her. With Anthony right next to her, Maria—after her heart had skipped a couple of beats, and laughing at herself for getting scared—replied sarcastically, "Oh shit, did see you that? Hmm, I wonder who this is." Giggling and carrying on as she did so, Maria answered the phone. "Hello."

Juanita, not recognizing Maria's voice (due to her laughter), demanded, "Who the fuck is this?" Realizing what Juanita was thinking right away, and quickly putting out the fire, Maria responded, "Easy there, it's just me. I was laughing 'cause I was just reaching for the phone to call your house, and it rang, scaring the shit out of me." Embarrassed by her outburst, and yet relieved at the same time, Juanita responded, "Ooh, I'm sorry. I didn't recognize your voice for minute there. I thought—" Not allowing Juanita to finish, talking low and walking away so that Anthony couldn't hear her, Maria replied, "Yeah, I know what you thought. Trust me, I would never let that happen. And I don't think you should say that to him right now, if you know what I mean." Shamefully, and agreeing, Juanita responded, "I know. You're right. So, is he alright? Am I still in the doghouse?" Walking back into the kitchen where Anthony awaited patiently, Maria answered, "Na, you're alright. I explained what happened. Look, Juanita, I'm sorry—this was all my fault. That was a stupid idea on my part, but I smoothed everything out for you. How are you doin'? Are you alright?" Having that big weight lifted off her shoulders and able to breathe normally again, Juanita now calmly answered, "I'm alright now that you told me that. And don't worry, Maria, it's not your fault. You had no way of knowing he'd react that way. To tell you the truth, neither did I. I should have thought about it a little before I agreed. Thank you so much for your help. I really owe you one. I don't know what I would have done if I lost him." Still feeling guilty, Maria replied, "No, please, Juanita. It was the least I could do. And as far as losing him, you know I would never allow that. I wouldn't be able to live with myself. Imagine what would happen to me if I caused the breakup of such a perfect couple. I would be sent to hell. I had to make it right. Here, you want to talk to him?" Able to joke about it now, Juanita said, "Na, that's okay. I'll talk to him whenever." Laughing along, not taking Juanita seriously, Maria replied, "Yeah, alright. Hang on. I'll see you in a few, right? You are coming here, right?" Insecurely, not knowing the answer, Juanita responded, "I don't know. I guess it will depend on him." Answering Juanita's last statement confidently, Maria replied, "Please. Okay, I'll see you in a little while, then. Hang on." Holding her hand over the speaker, Maria handed the phone to Anthony. Speaking low, yet demandingly, Maria said, "Anthony, here. Don't fuck this up, okay?

Anthony didn't say anything until Maria walked away. Once alone, Anthony swallowed, then spoke into the phone. "Babe, I am so—" Without allowing him to finish, Juanita quickly interrupted, "Wait, baby, don't say it. Don't say nothing yet. This one is my fault. I'm the one who is sorry. What I did was stupid, it was immature, and I don't have any good excuse for it. All I can say is that I am truly, truly sorry. And I promise you, if you take me back I will never do anything like this again." Refusing to let Juanita take all the blame, Anthony replied, "Take you back? What do you mean, take you back? Look, sweetheart, I was angry, yeah. But I didn't break up with you." Are you crazy? I would never let you go." Touched by Anthony's response and relieved, Juanita explained, "I'm saying though, when I saw that tear in your eye, and you run off like that, I'd swear it was all over. I never saw you like that before. It really scared me. I mean, we fought before, but you never left me like that before."

Feeling guilty himself now, this time Anthony interrupted, "I know, I know, baby. That is why I am sorry. It shouldn't have mattered what you did; I should not have left you like that. Of course you are going to think the worst after that. Na, the mature thing to do in that spot was to stay there and talk it out, and I ran away like a big baby. Na, babe, I was wrong. I'm really sorry, and I promise—no, I guarantee—that will never happen again. And, na—really, Juanita—I need to start acting like a man." Portraying her difference of opinion as to who was at fault, Juanita insisted, "Well, talking about maturity, I am almost two years older than you and I'm still playing games like a little kid. Look, baby, you were right. When I look back at everything we been through together, and everything you did for me, I have no reason to doubt your love. I do not need proof of your loyalty, and I certainly have no reason not to trust you."

Wanting to end the discussion and make up already, Anthony concluded, "Well, okay then, we're both sorry for what we did and we won't do it again. Let's forget about it. Let's just put this night behind us and move on with our lives, together." Unsatisfied by making up with just words and attempting to hint for an invite, Juanita, using her wit, said, "I still feel bad, though." Encouragingly, Anthony replied, "Don't, babe, it's over—don't even think about it anymore." Like playing chess, but using her words instead of chess pieces to acquire her goal, Juanita answered, "I can't stop thinking about it. We were having a good night until I fucked up. I won't feel better until I make it right."

Finally catching Juanita's hint, and deciding to play along, Anthony asked, "Well, what can you do now? I mean, do you know a way you can fix tonight?" With the make-up sex on her mind, Juanita—using her signature horny voice—replied, "Ooh, I know a lot of ways, but I will need your assistance. Would you like to help me?" Now sure of Juanita's intent, Anthony—continuing to play along—said, "Sure, I'll help. I'm listening. Why don't you explain to me what you need, in detail?"

Feeling things were back to normal and insuring her invite, Juanita played phone sex operator with Anthony. Knowing exactly what gets Anthony going, Juanita began by describing in detail the oral sex she was going to perform on him, how long she was going to do it for, and how many times. As Anthony got excited, he yearned for Juanita to tell him more. The more Juanita got into it, the more Anthony asked, "Then what?" Without further ado, an overexcited Anthony instructed, "Okay, enough talk. What are you waiting for? Hurry up and get over here." Without a second thought, Juanita—finally reaching her goal—responded, "I was just waiting for your permission and for the invite." Encouragingly Anthony replied, "You don't need my permission, or an invite. I belong to you. You can have me anytime you want. Now stop wasting time and get over here." Honoring Anthony's wish, Juanita answered excitedly, "Okay, baby, I'll be right there. I love you, baby." Off the phone, Juanita turned to her brother. "Where the fuck is the cab?" With a puzzled look on his face, Miguel regretfully answered, "It came, but I had to let him go." Not angry, yet very disappointed, Juanita asked, "Why? How come you ain't get me?" Indecisively, Miguel answered, "I didn't know what you wanted to do. I saw you on the phone, and it looked like you were talking seriously. I didn't want to disturb your conversation." Unable now to control her emotions, an upset Juanita responded, "Shit! I wish you would've said something. How long ago was this? When is the next one coming?" Observing Juanita uptight and feeling bad about it, Miguel apologetically replied, "I'm sorry, baby girl. I'm too drunk and fucked up to think, so when the cab got here I didn't know what to do. So I told him to go ahead. He said there won't be another one available for about an hour." Distressed now, Juanita impulsively yelled, "An hour? Fuck, I can't wait an hour! Why so long?" In an effort to calm Juanita down, and curious why she was so uptight, Miguel responded, "Because it's Friday night, all the clubs are closing, and everybody's trying to get a cab to go home. Why? What happened? Is everything alright?" With mixed feelings of anguish and anger, yet trying to avoid her older brother from feeling bad, Juanita answered, "Yeah, everything is okay now. Actually it is more than okay. Me and Anthony made up, but I need to get over there and do it the right way." Knowing exactly how Juanita was feeling and wanting to help her out, Miguel replied, "Man, I'm sorry. I fucked up. I didn't know you were gonna go there tonight. I thought we had time, that you were going there tomorrow." Really looking forward to see Anthony, a distressed Juanita consoled Miguel by saying, "Don't worry. I'm sorry, you didn't know. It's not your fault. I just don't know what to do now. Fuck it. Miguel, you feel like walking me?"

Believing that he owed Anthony for many reasons and wanting to contribute to Anthony and Juanita's happiness, Miguel brainstormed. Shaking his head in disagreement with his sister's request, Miguel responded, "Na, fuck that; that will take just as long. Wait here Juanita. I'll get a car."

Miguel wasn't the smartest man, nor was he the strongest man. He really didn't have a lot going for him at all. But the one thing he could do—his biggest talent—was to steal cars. One of the fastest car thieves around, Miguel mainly stole cars for money. Doing so professionally, Miguel never stole a car except to sell it. Never stealing a car when he was drinking, neither did Miguel ever bring his little sister into a stolen car. Going against his better judgment, and wanting to please Juanita, Miguel made an exception this time.

Although she didn't approve of his methods of taking care of her and their mother, Juanita always respected Miguel and never tried to stop him from stealing cars. That is why, minutes later, when Miguel pulled up in a stolen Honda, Juanita didn't object to getting in. Also, desperate to be with Anthony tonight and having complete faith in her older brother, it didn't even phase Juanita that Miguel was drunk.

As the remaining events of the night unfold, the opinions

of the outcome will vary depending on every individual's belief. Those who believe in God, in faith, and in destiny, would argue that the outcome was just meant to be. Believing that everything that happened on this particular day was determined from the moment the two lovers decided to go out—the argument, the decision to make up, and the means of transportation all belonged to the Almighty's ultimate plan. Instead of Juanita and Miguel being responsible for their own actions, is it easier to accept that a higher power had been involved? Or had there been too many coincidences happening this day to believe otherwise? Examining the night closely, one could blame fate for all the first-time occurrences. However, Juanita's, Miguel's, and Anthony's decisions could be blamed as well. Did God decide for Anthony and Juanita to go out on this night? Or did the two decide this for themselves? Did fate decide that Diane and Lisa— both of whom coincidentally resembled Miss Evans—to hit on Anthony? Or was it due to Juanita leaving Anthony alone in a club—the reason the girls made their attempt? Who prevented Juanita from stepping in while the girls attempted to pick up Anthony? Maria? Juanita herself? Or did Anthony's witholding of information about his experience with Miss Evans play a part? Maybe if she knew, Juanita would have interrupted sooner, the argument would have been prevented, and everyone would have gone home safely together. Was it destiny that missed their cab, got into a vulnerable stolen car, and then drive it drunk? Whatever it was that controlled the outcome—fate, destiny, God, or even Anthony and Juanita themselves—one thing is certain. Just as no decision they made could have foreseen the future, nothing Anthony and Juanita did could have changed the past.

Having stolen dozens of cars in the past, this would be the first time Miguel had ever done it for just a ride. Never stealing a car that wasn't worth money, or was durable, this would also be the first time Miguel stole a car while he was drunk and stoned. Because of the circumstances—stealing the car for convenience only—Miguel chose that particular Honda Civic because it was parked just around the corner and it was a synch to take. Little could Miguel foresee the tragedy that, by making his choice and bringing Juanita into it, would change the lives of those involved forever.

While driving Juanita to see Anthony, high on alcohol and marijuana, Miguel was convinced a police car was following him. He constantly looked through the rearview mirror, and so—not paying attention to the road ahead—drove right through a red stoplight. With no time—and certainly no reflexes—for Miguel to bail, an old and heavy Chevy Impala barreled through Juanita's side of the undermatched Honda they were in. Although the Chevy wasn't traveling at a high speed, because of its size the impact caused the Honda to spin out of control into a couple of parked cars nearby. Miguel and Juanita were both knocked unconscious, the door to the Honda was crushed inward, and Juanita had been impaled through her lower back and liver.

After being treated for minor injuries, worried about his little sister's condition, Miguel asked the doctor, "Where's my sister?" In an effort to keep Miguel calm, yet urgently needing to explain, the doctor answered, "Your sister is in ICU. She is in critical condition. I'm afraid it is very serious." With a heavy heart and tears in his eyes, Miguel asked, "Is she gonna be alright?" Sparing Miguel from a breakdown, yet disclosing everything at the same time, the doctor responded, "We are doing everything we can for her. Right now she is still unconscious, and it is best that she rest. If there is anyone you need to call, like your parents, I suggest you do so now."

7:00 Saturday morning, taking the Doctor's advice, Miguel found the nearest payphone and called his mother. Sandra—a strong, religious Mexican woman—answered the phone, "Hello." Hearing his mother's voice and unable to stay calm, Miguel informed her, "Ma, there's been a terrible accident. You need to come to the hospital right away." Becoming instantly worried, yet wanting more information, Sandra inquired, "Easy, Miguel, calm down. Tell me what happened—slowly." After explaining the incident and Juanita's condition to his mother, Miguel instructed her, "Ma, Anthony doesn't know what happened. He's at his friend Vincent's house. I have Vincent's number written down in the phonebook on my dresser. Do me a favor, please? Call Anthony and tell him? Thanks." Considering Anthony to be her son in law and having great admiration for him, Sandra agreed. "Absolutely."

Because it had been two hours and his girl had not arrived, Anthony had been sitting right next to the phone when Sandra called. Knowing Juanita, and feeling something was wrong, Anthony urgently answered once the phone rang. "Hello!" Surprising Anthony by calling, yet not wasting any time, Sandra quickly informed him, "Anthony, Juanita's in the hospital. I'm afraid there was a bad accident." Frozen by the news, unable to speak coherently, Anthony inquired, "What. What happened? Is she okay? Where? Truly not knowing what to say to him, Sandra replied, "Anthony, I don't know much. I am going over there now." Without thinking twice, Anthony replied urgently, "That's okay, Ma, I'll see you there. Thank you for calling."

Arriving at the hospital, Anthony was greeted by Miguel in the lobby. Eliminating the small chitchat and getting right to the point, Anthony asked, "Where is she? Is she alright?"

Miguel led him to Juanita's room and informed him, "She's awake now, but she's in really bad shape."

As Anthony entered her room and rushed to her side, Juanita began to cry hysterically. Attempting to speak, with a crackling in her voice, she said, "I'm so sor—"

Holding Juanita tightly in his arms, and comforting her the best he could, Anthony said, "Shhh, baby, don't speak. It's okay, I'm with you now. I'm with you now forever." Observing the scene and touched by it, Sandra, who arrived to the hospital minutes before Anthony, began crying as well. Continuing to hold Juanita, and fighting back his tears, insuring her, Anthony replied, "It's okay, sweetheart. You're gonna be alright."

After a few moments, and everyone halfway calmed, Juanita looked at Anthony sadly and said, "Baby, I have to tell you something." In an effort to have Juanita relax and conserve her energy, Anthony responded, "Babe, whatever it is, tell me later. You need to rest now." Juanita, shaking her no, continued to attempt to speak yet—because he wanted her to rest—kept getting interrupted by Anthony. Finally, building up enough strength, Juanita—raising her voice—demandingly instructed, "Babe! Thank you, but I don't want to rest now. You need to know something—it is very important." Juanita having his complete attention, and continuing to comfort and relax her, Anthony curiously inquired, "Okay, babe, easy. What is it?" As the tears rolled down her face, Juanita—attempting to be tough about it—replied, "Anthony, I need a new liver—mine is no good. If I don't get one soon, I am gonna die."

Dropping to his knees, as his heart did to his stomach, Anthony—breaking down crying and looking towards God—shouted, "No! No! Why? This can't be happening. There's gotta be a mistake. Please, God, tell me it's a mistake." Assisted by Sandra, Juanita pulled Anthony towards her. He buried his face in her breast; crying along with Anthony, Juanita pleaded, "Ahr, babe. Please relax. Please don't make it harder for me." As Anthony—jumpy and trying to escape her hold—attempted to resist Juanita, Juanita just held him tight. Holding Anthony for a few minutes until he surrendered, and speaking more softly, Juanita repeated her pleas and added, "Babe, please. I need you to be strong. I can't do this without you."

With a few heavy breaths, Anthony, once he calmed his nerves, said, "Okay, babe. I'm sorry. What can I do? I feel I need to do something."

In an effort to fill Anthony in with all the details, Juanita informingly said, "There is nothing you can do. There is nothing anyone can do. They need to find a matching liver for me soon. The odds of that happening are slim. Anthony, make me a promise. Keep me awake as much as possible, and promise you will stay with me until—" Moving his face towards Juanita's, looking her in the eyes and kissing her lips repeatedly between each of his sentences, Anthony promised, "Don't worry, baby. I promise I ain't going nowhere. And don't give up. If we can stop this from happening, we will. I am gonna talk to the doctors, specialists, or whoever I have to. Please just hang in there. I love you so much. And I am gonna be with you every minute you are here. Promise."

After laying in Juanita's arms until she fell asleep, Anthony—exhausted as well—stayed true to his word. Along with Sandra, trying to gather as much information as he could, Anthony talked desperately to all the doctors possible. Though their opinions varied, the bottom line was the same: The damage sustained by Juanita's liver was irreversible. If Juanita did not get a new liver, the machines would only prolong the inevitable failure of her own.

Sandra, Miguel and Anthony all checked to see if any of their livers would be usable. None of them were compatible—but even if they had been, Juanita would not have allowed any of them to exchange their life for hers. The only hope Juanita had was to find a compatible donor who died for reasons not related to liver failure.

The news of Juanita's condition spread throughout the neighborhood the day after the accident. As the other visitors just came and went, Maria and Vincent—the first two to know—stayed with Anthony and Juanita every day. Maybe it was seeing all these people that made Juanita sad, or maybe she knew her time was near; however, Juanita just wanted time alone with Anthony. Whatever the case might have been, it caused Juanita to summon Anthony to come closer to her. Heavily medicated, Juanita—whispering in Anthony's ear—instructed, "Do me a favor. Get rid of everyone. I wanna be alone." Kissing Juanita's forehead, then retreating to honor her request, Anthony announced, "Look everyone, thank you for coming. We appreciate it. I'm sorry, but Juanita's tired and she needs some rest. Let's leave her alone for a while."

Raising no objections whatever as they departed the room one by one, everyone wished Anthony and Juanita the best. Once everyone else had left, and Anthony was still standing near the door, Sandra sat down next to Juanita on her bed. Looking towards Anthony and speaking so he wouldn't be offended, Juanita requested, "Baby, do me a favor? Let me talk to my mommy alone for a minute." Respectfully, Anthony nodded his head yes and removed himself from the room.

With nothing to lose, Juanita—looking for her mother's

blessing—explained, "Ma, you know how I feel about Anthony, right?" Just listening, not saying a word, Sandra allowed Juanita to say what she already knew her daughter was going to. Nervous, yet determined, Juanita respectfully continued. "Me and Anthony been together a long time. And we also had been together intimately all this time too. Since you know this now, I was wondering—I mean, I was thinking—since—" Observing Juanita having trouble asking for her last request, Sandra interrupted her. Knowing exactly what was on her daughter's mind, Sandra was proud of herself for raising such a respectful young lady. Without Juanita needing to finish, Sandra gave her blessing by saying, "Yes, Juanita, you may." While doing so, Sandra—noticing that Juanita was ashamed—had been waiting for the moment to have this woman-to-woman talk since her baby girl was born. Without further ado, Sandra said, "Look, baby, I'm old, but I am not stupid. I know of all your relations with Anthony. Did you really think I didn't know? You are your mother's daughter. Anthony is an incredibly gorgeous man. Only a fool would think you didn't sleep with him by now. If it was me, I would have gave it up to him in less than a month."

With the ice broken, Juanita, feeling relieved, laughed at her mother's statement and said, "Then it's true. Me and you do think the same. From the moment I met him, I knew he was the one. And even though he was the first, I didn't waste any time holding out. Anthony just makes me so—well, you know." Understanding exactly what Juanita meant, Sandra continued, "Well if that is how you feel, why do you feel you need my permission now?" Thinking about it a moment, Juanita replied, "It's not so much permission I was looking for, or even your blessing. I mean, it's a little late for that now. Besides, I assumed I already had both anyway. What I need really is your advice. This may be the last chance I get to be with him, Do you think it is appropriate to do it in here? How do I go about getting Anthony to do it too?"

Happy in the display of confidence her only daughter had shown in her, Sandra proudly advised, "Juanita, I'm glad you came to me with this. I'm glad to see I raised you right—that under the circumstances you would even consider getting my approval. But Juanita, really. This is no time to worry about what other people think. To tell you the truth, I would have given anything to be with your father just one more time before he passed. And Anthony, it's obvious how much he loves you. Even if the situation wasn't what it is, he's the kind of man that if you tell him what you want, he just does it. It is very rare to have a man like that." Kissing Juanita on the forehead, and caressing her cheek, Sandra took a deep sigh of pride. Concluding her advice, Sandra added, "Matter of fact, there is nothing else to talk about. We're wasting valuable time. I'll send him in, and I'll see you later."

Retreating outside the room, ignoring everyone else's questions about Juanita—only focused on honoring her baby's need—Sandra went up to Anthony. Putting her hands on his, Sandra kissed Anthony's cheek and whispered softly in his ear, "Thank you for making her so happy. She wants you in there." Smiling now, she added, "Go get 'im, tiger."

Red from embarrassment, Anthony could only say, "Okay."

"Babe, do me a favor," Juanita told him as he entered. "Close the door behind you." Nervous—as though it would be their first time—she added, "Lock it too."

"Okay." Making his way to her side, he asked, "Babe, are you okay? Do you need anything?" With only one thing on her mind—following her mother's advice and not wasting any time—Juanita replied, "Yeah. Matter of fact I do. It will make me feel a lot better." Knowing exactly what Juanita was talking about, Anthony, playing along, inquired, "Oh yeah? What's that?" Answering Anthony by grabbing his crotch, then using her signature sex voice, Juanita replied, "Well, I believe I owe you something." Wanting very much to please Juanita, yet uncertain how safe it was, Anthony inquired, "Do you think this is a good idea?" Being concerned only about her mother's opinion, Juanita—slightly uptight—answered, "I don't care. Please, Anthony. I need you now. Please don't deny me. Not now." Knowing exactly how Juanita must have felt just then,

Anthony—so as not to spoil the mood—responded quickly. "No, of course not. Your wish is my command. Only I am doing the work—you just lay back and enjoy it." Objecting to Anthony's consideration, Juanita replied, "Umm, umm, no way. I'm gonna make sure you never forget me."

Afterward, Juanita laid on Anthony's chest. They spoke of the past—only of their love for each other.

Finally Anthony said, "Maybe we should get dressed now. Are you ready for your company?" Satisfied sexually, Juanita—laying naked in Anthony's arms and purring like a kitten—replied, "Ahrrr, I don't want to. Can't I just stay right here? They can still come in if they want." Liking Juanita's idea better, yet trying to avoid being rude, Anthony responded, "No, it wouldn't be right. We owe it to them—at least to your mother, anyway." Letting out a sigh of both agreement and annoyance, Juanita replied, "Alright. You're right—go ahead."

While getting dressed, and helping Juanita put her robe on, Anthony observed the anguish on the love of his life's face. Feeling bad for Juanita, and trying to lift her spirits, Anthony promised, "Babe, I promise, once everyone leaves, we'll do it again if you want." Her face lighting up with joy, an excited Juanita inquired, "All night?" Keeping her happiness going, Anthony kissed Juanita on the lips and agreed, "All night." No longer moping, Juanita—with a sense of urgency—instructed, "Okay, babe—chop, chop. Hurry up now. The faster they come in, the faster they can go out."

Juanita accepted the entire visitation and greeted her friends accordingly. Most people facing death would not have been able to stay so cheerful, but Juanita was strong. Even with their sorrow and pity, and surrounded by her friends and family, their love kept Juanita high in spirit. Juanita only became her saddest when she thought of leaving Anthony behind. She only wanted to spend as much time as she could with him. So she counted the minutes until visiting hours were over.

Seeing how Juanita kept watch on the clock, Sandra decided to help her daughter out by dropping a hint. Looking at her watch, Sandra said aloud, "Wow, look how late it is. I didn't realize the time."

It was a noble attempt—but since none of the company worked, or had anything to do the following morning, time was not a factor for them. But after seeing Juanita curl up in Anthony's arms oblivious to everyone else, Maria caught on.

Catching Sandra's hint and helping to spread it around, Maria agreed and said aloud, "Yeah, she's right. It is late. We should really get outta here."

Slowly but surely, wishing her well, all of Anthony and Juanita's friends departed for the night—last but not least among them Sandra. On her way out, addressing her daughter, Sandra said happily, "Juanita, I am so proud of you. I know it was really hard to deal with all those people when you just want to be alone. It was the right thing to do." Then, referring to Anthony, she added, "Well, it looks like you are in good hands tonight. I love you. I'll see you in the morning." Because of the lack of attention and respect displayed towards her mother, Anthony smacked Juanita lovingly on the buttocks and stared at her disappointingly. Looking at Anthony's face and realizing what she did, Juanita changed her mindset for the moment and directed her attention towards her mother. Embarrassed by her own rudeness, Juanita apologetically replied, "Oh my God, I'm sorry, ma. I love you too. Thank you for everything. Really. I'll see you in the morning." Laughing at her daughter getting disciplined, Sandra instructed, "That's a good boy Anthony. You keep her in line. Watch her, too, she's just like me when I was her age."

"Very funny," Juanita said. "Just lock the door on your way out."\

As anticipated, the moment everyone left, Anthony and Juanita engaged in the all-nighter that was promised. In the small hours of the morning, lying on top of Anthony as she was accustomed, Juanita was no longer her usual gleeful self.

Feeling her time was near, Juanita opened up the conversation very glumly. Thinking about her fate, Juanita asked, Why did this have to happen? We're good people."

Hearing Juanita's words caused tears to develop in Anthony's eyes. He tried to make sense of it, but Anthony could not think of an answer. Crying, he said, "I wish I could tell you babe. I wanna know myself. All I know is life ain't fair. It really makes me wonder too—why do the right thing when at any time something bad could happen for no reason?" Getting worried seeing Anthony like this, Juanita asked, "What are you gonna do? Baby, please promise me you won't do nothing stupid." No longer crying—but the tears still in his eyes—Anthony responded, "Juanita, I can't promise you nothin. You're still here but I don't know how I'm gonna be after." In an effort to ease the tension, Juanita—playing around now—asked jokingly, "Are you gonna find another girl?" His first reaction was to answer honestly and offensively; but to play along with Juanita's game, Anthony replied, "Of course. I have one in mind right now. I figured I'd invite her to your funeral as our first date." Realizing that Anthony's sadistic humor in play, Juanita smacked him on the stomach and replied, "Stop playing. Really—do you think you will ever be with someone else?"

Obviously, under the circumstances Anthony never gave thought to being in another relationship. The last thing anyone could think about when faced with losing his or her soulmate is finding another. The only answer Anthony could give Juanita is the one that came from his heart. Unpracticed, speaking only how he felt, Anthony answered, "Juanita, I'll tell you the truth. I really believe true love happens only once in a lifetime. I'd never thought I'd fall in love until I met you. Then when we were together, I knew we were made for each other. I can't see me loving anyone like this again. You are the perfect girl, Juanita. What are the chances that I will find that again?" Satisfied by Anthony's answer, yet attempting to reassure him, Juanita replied, "I think you will. You are a great guy, Anthony, and you're gonna make some girl very happy. And it's alright. Because the truth is, I'll be dead and you'll have your whole life ahead of you. But do me a favor. Promise me you will only be with someone who appreciates you. Someone who will return all the happiness you give." By this time Anthony had already nodded off. After being awake and running around for the last three days, then taking care of his sexual duties, everything finally caught up with Anthony. Noticing Anthony falling asleep, Juanita took the gold chain and crucifix off her neck and put it on his. Kissing his lips, she whispered in his ear. "Thank God for you."

Laying back on top of Anthony with her head on his chest, Juanita fell asleep too.

The next morning when he awoke, Anthony noticed Juanita's chain on his neck. Anthony woke Juanita in his usual romantic fashion—kissing her on the neck and upper breast. Smiling as she opened her eyes, Juanita greeted Anthony, "Morning, baby." Returning the greeting by whispering in Juanita's ear, Anthony said, "Morning, sweetheart. I am sorry for waking you. Why did you put your chain on me?" Still smiling in delight, Juanita responded to both of Anthony's statements. Talking as if she felt uncomfortable, Juanita replied, "I gave you my chain so you will always remember me. But na, I'm glad you woke me. I don't want to waste too much time sleeping anyway." Being offended by what Juanita said, Anthony responded defensively, "What? Babe I'm gonna remember you always anyway. I don't need your chain. I gave it to you." Being agitated from Anthony's response, and for rejecting her gesture, Juanita demanded, "I know. This is why it is so special. Look, Anthony, I don't need it anymore, and you do. Please just keep it. I want that—everytime you look at it, you will remember me. Please, babe! Just do it." Even if the circumstances were not what they were, Anthony—as he usually did—gave in and responded, "Okay, fine, I'm not gonna argue with you." Spoiled by Anthony, and accustomed to always getting her way, Juanita very confidently responded, "Good boy. You know better than to argue with me anyway. Now give me a kiss and hand me my robe. I have to pee." Giving Juanita her robe, then following up with a series of kisses on her lips, Anthony and Juanita were interrupted when Sandra entered the room.

"Hello. Company is here," Sandra said awkwardly. "Don't

yous ever take a break? I'm surprised I don't have twenty grandchildren already."

"Hi, Company," Juanita said. "It only looks like we're doing something all the time. Maybe it's just that you have bad timing." Smirking at her daughter's wisecrack, Sandra replied, "Please, Juanita. Who you think you're foolin? I have bad timing because poor Anthony is too good looking. Besides being worn out, how are you feeling anyway?"

Assisted to her feet by Anthony, Juanita said, "A little dizzy there. I'm okay, though—a little weak, my stomach hurts a little, but okay." Continuing to attempt to embarrass her daughter—and, inadvertently, Anthony—with her sexual remarks, Sandra said, "Hmm, good going, Anthony. He really knocks you out, huh? Where was he thirty years ago when I was your age?" Complimenting her man and setting her mother straight, Juanita—grinning as she spoke—responded, "Yeah, actually he does. But that's not it. I think I'm getting my period. Matter of fact let me use the bathroom, I'll be right out."

After helping Juanita to the bathroom, Anthony returned to Sandra and engaged in a conversation with her. Without hesitating and showing her appreciation, Sandra began the conversation by saying, "Thank you so much for you. Even now, while she is in her last days, anyone else would be going crazy. But since she has you, she can pass on a happy woman. There are people out there that go through their whole life never experiencing what you two have. So although Juanita's life will be short, because of you it is never empty. So, Anthony, thank you. Thank you so much." Observing the sadness in her words, Anthony—giving Sandra a strong hug, responded, "There is no reason to thank me, Ma. Really, she made me just as happy, if not more. Me and Juanita just talked about this last night. She asked me if I would ever be with someone else. And I answered her. It doesn't matter if never find love again. Like you said, people go through their whole life without ever having what I had with Juanita. And even though mine was cut short, I still have to thank God for blessing m—"

It could not have not been written any more dramatically

than the way it actually happened. If Anthony had doubted the existence of God before, he doubted no longer. He could not explain it any other way—from being given one more night with Juanita to being handed a chain and crucifix by the near-departed love of his life, to even mentioning God himself the very moment God was claiming Juanita's soul. For no sooner did Anthony finishing thanking God than a loud high pitch scream coming from the bathroom echoed through the room.

Without acknowledging her mother's presence, Juanita cried out, "Anthony! Come quick!"

Rushing to the bathroom and bursting through the locked door, Anthony discovered Juanita lying on the floor in a pool of blood. Lifting Juanita's body, he turned to Sandra and said, "Call a doctor."

While Anthony carried Juanita's body to the bed, Sandra immediately followed his instructions. At the moment Juanita's liver had failed and her life was slipping away, Anthony—feeling helpless and looking towards God—cried aloud, "No! Please, God, no! I'm not ready for this!" As she laid there unconscious, yet still breathing, Anthony—speaking to Juanita's motionless body—pleaded, "Hold on, baby. Don't leave me now. Please baby, wake up. Wake up!"

Approaching her bedside, a doctor instructed Anthony, "Okay, let us work now. You need to move away."

Disregarding the doctor's orders, too anxious to be calmed, Anthony continued trying to wake Juanita. The doctor had to order security to assist in removing Anthony. Juanita was moved to another room, and Sandra assisted in trying to calm Anthony.

He was still pinned by the security guards and screaming to be let go when Sandra barked, "Let him go. I got it from here." Kneeling down and holding her daughter's man in her arms, Sandra consoled him. "It's okay, baby. They'll take care of her from here. Don't worry—they'll save her. She's going to be alright." Not having any faith in the doctors whatsoever, Anthony hysterically cried back, "No! She needs me in there! She won't respond to them! She'll only respond to me! They got to let me in there, they got to let me in!" Agreeing with Anthony, yet cooperating with the hospital's policy, Sandra—holding him tighter now—replied, "I know, baby, I know. But we can't. But don't worry, Anthony. God is in there with her. God is with her."

After about an hour—Anthony and Sandra still awaiting the news of Juanita's fate—the doctor entered. He did not need to say a word. The look on his face made it clear that it was over. Before allowing the doctor to explain the diagnosis, Sandra had already buried her face in Anthony's chest. Holding her hand up towards the doctor in the stop position, not wanting to hear the "we did everything we could" cliché, Sandra instructed, "No, don't say it. Please just don't."

Crying alongside Sandra, Anthony turned to the doctor and said, "I'm sorry but we need to be alone right now. This is still too hard, you know?" Completely respectful, the doctor replied, "By all means. Take all the time you need. Whenever you're ready, I'll help you with anything you need."

As predicted, Juanita's passing changed the lives of everyone who had been close to her. After the initial shock of Juanita's death was over, and all the funereal duties were behind, many negative events would follow.

Miguel, unable to forgive himself for ultimately being responsible for causing his sister's death, committed suicide just a couple of weeks later.

Sandra, with both of her children gone, no longer had any reason to continue living in the United States. Transporting the remains of her children, as well as her late husband's, and leaving everything else behind, she returned to Mexico to be near her relatives. The dream of a better life in America, promised by Sandra's husband, would eventually become a nightmare.

With their top member passing, The Mutts would soon dismantle.

As for Anthony, there is still much more to be written. After Juanita's death, Anthony's life—to no one's surprise—took a turn for the worse. To suppress the emptiness left by Juanita's passing, Anthony sought love by turning to drugs. When pot and alcohol no longer had any effect he started dropping acid—which (if any are) is certainly not the right drug for a man in mourning. Acid alters the personality from depression to giddiness—but guilty now from the happiness the acid had inflicted, Anthony searched for an alternate means of getting high and turned to cocaine. Just as anyone would when beginning to use cocaine, Anthony first started by sniffing it. Coming from an alcoholic father, taking dependencies to that extent was in Anthony's genes. Once his naval cavities got clogged to the point he could no longer sniff the cocaine, he began to smoke it. In the days before crack, cocaine could be smoked when it was cooked up with baking soda and water and its compound was thus altered to a purer form. Known as "freebase," Anthony smoked it for days at a time. It was not that Anthony enjoyed the high from smoking freebase, but the addiction overwhelmed his willpower. And once again, freebase—which can keep you awake and paranoid for days—was not the drug to keep Anthony's mind off Juanita. It isn't wise to do something that will keep you awake for days. Searching still, then, for an escape from reality, Anthony turned to PCP, or "Angel Dust," as it is known on the street. But he would use it just once. When he awoke in the parked car of a stranger, with no clue how he got there, he determined he would never smoke it again.

At last, Anthony settled on heroin. Never going as far as to use it intravenously, Anthony became addicted to heroin just by sniffing it. Soon after becoming addicted, Anthony returned a favor to his brother for turning him on to marijuana by turning Joseph on to heroin as well. It was the high they were both looking for; and Anthony and Joseph did heroin every day, every chance they had. Still selling pot to support his habit, Anthony continued sniffing heroin until a few years later it got out of hand. When the habit began costing him $200 a day, Anthony robbed the guys he was selling marijuana for, and thereafter had to disappear from the neighborhood. With a price now on his head, Anthony stole everything he could to support his addiction. He tried many times to quit, but due to the overbearing withdrawal symptoms he couldn't put it down.

After praying to God for guidance, Anthony's addiction finally came to an end after he and Joseph were arrested for stealing a car. His first child on the way, Joseph—in an effort to support his family—had just signed up with the Navy before getting arrested. Since a criminal record would have destroyed any chance in the Navy Joseph had, Anthony decided to take sole responsibility for the crime. It was a noble gesture, but as a result Joseph would never learn to be responsible for his own actions. After Anthony threw himself at the mercy of the court, the judge, instead of sending him to jail, sentenced him to complete a substance abuse program, and after about two and a half years he completed his rehabilitation. While there, Anthony learned alternative ways of coping with the experiences that plagued his life. Meeting people that had their own skeletons to let out, Anthony discovered he was not alone. Still very private, though, and believing it was irrelevant to his drug addiction, Anthony still never told anyone about Miss Evans and the effect she had on him, but he was finally able to let go of Juanita and open himself to love again—hence filling positively the empty gap left by Juanita's passing, just like she wanted him to.

With limited work experience and a criminal record, it wasn't easy for Anthony to find a job. But with six months and the help of Richard Jeter, an acquaintance from rehab, Anthony got a job at an overnight shipping company in the city. In the thirteen years that followed, Anthony would move up the ranks in the company and become manager of the New Jersey branch.

At the beginning of his employment, Anthony worked beside Richard and became good friends with him. When Richard had broken up with his girlfriend and needed help to pay his bills, he asked Anthony to become roommate. Skeptical at first, but feeling he owed Richard for getting him the job, Anthony agreed. Two young single guys, both of whom were now looking for love, made the most of their bachelor pad. After moving in together, Anthony and Richard—in order to accomplish their quest of finding that significant other—began going out to clubs every weekend. They both had trouble—it had been a long time since either had been socially active in this way. With nothing to lose, Anthony called upon his old friends Vincent and Maria to show them the hot spots. Before long, all four began going out every weekend.

But meeting women who only had one-night stands on their minds made Anthony frustrated. After spending so much time together, Richard and Maria began dating, and Vincent fell in love with—and would eventually marry—the first girl he met. Since his friends were now involved in relationships, and there wasn't anyone to accompany him, Anthony gave up the club scene. As he was about to give up on love, believing that his one chance had passed along with Juanita, Anthony—in a desperate state of mind—would eventually make one of the biggest mistakes of his life.

One day, riding the train to work and deep in thought, Anthony had an aimless stare in his eyes. Anthony already having given up on his quest for love, into his life walked an overconfident Puerto Rican girl named Yvette. Without noticing her, and thinking about something else, Anthony was engaged in a blank stare in her direction. She had long black hair, slicked back in a ponytail, and wore contact lenses that had altered her eye color from brown to green. Taking his stare as a compliment, Yvette—in an attempt to make conversation—approached Anthony and asked, "Does this train go to 42nd Street?" Still occupied in thought, Anthony didn't respond at first to the buxom young woman. Quickly agitated, Yvette—repeating the question more snobbishly—asked, "Hello, excuse me. Can you tell me if this train goes to 42nd Street?"

His trance now broken, Anthony—embarrassed by his lack of attention—said, "Oh, I'm sorry. Were you talking to me?" Rolling her eyes and giving Anthony a look as if he were stupid, Yvette replied, "Yeah. I mean, you were staring right at me." Still embarrassed, and trying to be polite, Anthony inquired, "Really, was I staring? I'm sorry, I didn't mean to. I was thinking about something else. Your question—yeah, this train does go to 42nd Street."

It was the train she took home every day, and Yvette already knew the answer to her own question. Believing because of his stare that Anthony was interested in her, Yvette just used this question to approach him. Since she already knew that this train didn't stop at the station of inquiry, Yvete—pretending to be surprised by Anthony's answer, inquired, "Are you sure?" Confident in his knowledge, Anthony responded, "Yeah, of course. 42nd Street, Times Square, right?" Realizing the confusion, and embarrassed herself now, Yvette answered, "No, I'm sorry. I meant 42nd Street in Queens, not Manhattan." Having little knowledge of Queens, yet trying to be helpful, Anthony responded, "I'm sorry, I don't know nothin about Queens; but here—let's look at the map and see."

"Where are you from?" Yvette asked as they referred to the transit map.

Anthony gave Yvette a quick lookover and replied, "Me, I'm from Brooklyn. It doesn't look like this train goes to 42nd Street in Queens."

Paying little attention to the train schedule, Yvette—continuing her pick-up maneuvering—responded, "That's okay. I'm going somewhere else now anyway. You know Brooklyn is the other way? Do you know where you're going?" Realizing Yvette's scheme, Anthony intelligently played along and replied, "Yeah. I'm on my way to work, though." Delighted that Anthony had a job, Yvette curiously asked, "Oh really? What do you do?" Not proud of his occupation, Anthony hesitantly answered, "I work the late shift in a warehouse." Not really interested and just making small talk, Yvette implied, "Oh, that's good. At least you have a job—so many people these days can't find work anywhere." Remembering his struggles in his job search, Anthony agreed and replied, "Yeah, I know. I was looking for about six months before my friend got me in there. What do you do?" Nonchalant, non-caring, and unconcerned, Yvette answered, "Oh, I just go to school now. I just gave birth to my son not to long ago, so I really don't have time to work." Appearing too young to have children, Anthony—beating around the bush—responded, "Oh, congratulations. You and your husband must be really happy. Was that your first one?" Observing Anthony's motives, Yvette just spilled, "Na, I have a daughter who's three—I had her when I was sixteen, from a different father than my son's. I'm not married. My son's father is locked up and we're not together anymore. What about you? Married? Got kids? Girlfriend?" Surprised by Yvette's response, yet not wanting to seem judgmental, Anthony answered, "No, no, and no, I am all alone." Not believing Anthony about his status, Yvette inquired, "Yeah right. Looking like you do, you're trying to tell me you don't have no one. Why not?" Flattered by Yvette's compliment, Anthony smiled and replied, "Na, serious, it's a long story. I'd tell you about it, but I have to get off the next stop." Not yet satisfied with the conversation, Yvette inquired, "Really? You're gonna get off?"

Standing up, awaiting the train to arrive in the station, Anthony's intent was to get off. Without knowing this girl's name or her phone number, Anthony realized if he chose to get off right now, there would be a good chance he'd never see her again. Another example how one simple choice would, in turn, determine the future. Intrigued by the conversation, and wondering if this girl could be the one, Anthony changed his mind in a split second. Not wanting to feel the "what if" syndrome, Anthony, reconsidering, said, "Know what? I'm early. I could stay on a couple of more stops." Glad with his choice, yet not wanting show it, Yvette—acting conceited—asked, "What are you staying on for?" Building up his nerve, Anthony—realizing he had nothing to lose—explained his actions by saying, "Well, I was enjoying the conversation, and I was wondering if I could get your name and number so we could finish it maybe later." Hesitant to comply, Yvette made an excuse and responded, "My name is Yvette. I would give you my number, but the phone where I live is not really mine. But why don't you give me yours and I call you?"

Anthony provided the information with the idea he wouldn't hear from her. He figured that, having two kids, Yvette was looking for someone more financially secure. If she were to call him, Anthony believed it would be for only a one-night stand.

"It was nice meeting you Yvette," he said as the train pulled into the next station.

It should not have been a surprise that Yvette was single—although she had a beautiful face and an incredible body, Yvette had a horrible personality. She was 5'5"; had legs up to her neck and the steroetypically Puerto Rican, chunky, round butt; and 36D breasts that seemed to point up to God. She flaunted all these assets; and, after looking at her, most men were guaranteed to have her on their minds while they masturbated or had sex with their wives.

Yvette's flaw was her wicked attitude. Angry at the world, Yvette talked down to everybody. Never appreciating anything anyone did for her, Yvette always wanted more. Greed is ugly, but when selfishness and inconsideration are added, it can turn even the most beautiful person into a monster. Yvette never had trouble finding a boyfriend, but she did have trouble keeping a boyfriend. After learning how she carried herself, it was no wonder at all to Anthony why both Yvette's children's fathers walked out on such a gorgeous woman.

A few days after their meeting on the train, Yvette called Anthony. Upon learning he had no plans for the weekend, Yvette invited Anthony to come to her apartment on Saturday. Anthony suspected that Yvette was just looking to have sex with someone. And realizing her unpleasantness, Anthony considered that if there were anyone he could sleep with and then walk away from, it would be Yvette.

When he arrived at her apartment, Yvette—strangely—greeted Anthony with a hug and a small kiss on the lips.

Finding Yvette's greeting strange himself, Anthony said, "How are you doin?" It was obvious that Yvette wanted him there for something more than just company. For when answering Anthony's greeting, a distressed look appeared on Yvette's face as she responded, "Not so good. I'm having a lot of problems right now." Barely knowing Yvette and truthfully unconcerned, Anthony was just being polite when he inquired, "Why? What's the matter?" With no pride whatsoever, hinting so badly she might as well have come right out and asked, Yvette answered, "Well, my welfare check didn't come yet. My baby needs milk and diapers. My phone bill is due tomorrow, and if I can't get the money, they're gonna turn off my phone. So I've been really stressing." In an effort to help and offer some ideas, Anthony asked, "How much do you need? Can you get the money from your parents, or someone else in your family?"

Expecting that Anthony would have offered her the money, Yvette became upset when he didn't. Quickly turning from the warm, loving person who answered the door to cold and heartless, Yvette—like a deprived and spoiled child—responded, "Na, my phone bill is two hundred dollars, no one in my family has that kind of money. Look, I'm sorry for inviting you over, but I really don't want to hang out or be bothered with anybody. Don't expect me to call you either, since my phone will be off."

After how Yvette had just came off, most men—desperate for sex or not—would have walked out right there. Anthony was no different, standing there with a confused look, contemplating helping out this ill-tempered homecoming princess or walking out and never hearing from her again—a choice he knew he'd regret either way. Fortunately for Yvette, Anthony's mother was a single parent as well. Knowing how difficult it must be for Yvette, and having a soft spot in her heart for her, Anthony—annoyed as he did so—replied, "Look, Yvette, I could help you if you want. I mean, since we're not going out nowhere anyhow, I'll just give you the money." Relieved by Anthony's offering, Yvette—out of respect and pleasantly now—inquired, "Why? What do you mean?" Explaining his plan for the night, and now the alternate one, Anthony answered, "Well, I brought $250 with me. I was going to pay for a babysitter for you, take you to the Yankee game, to dinner, and maybe a little dancing later on. But since you don't want to do nothing with this stress on your mind, I figured I'd just as well give you the money. You understand what I'm saying? I was gonna spend that much on you anyway. But since you need to pay your bill more than you need a date, just take the money. Just don't say I never offered to take you out."

Accepting the money with no gratitude whatsoever, Yvette—happy that her plan worked—responded, "Well, that's okay, I'm not a big fan of baseball anyway." Making his way towards the door intending to leave, Anthony replied, "Then we're better off. I'll remember that if I ever get the chance to take you out again. I was glad I could help you out. Have a good night. Give me a call sometime."

Observing the disappointment in Anthony's face, and probably feeling a little guilty for using him, Yvette inquired, "Why are you leaving?" Being very proud and not wanting to impose, Anthony answered, "Because you said you don't feel like hanging out. Besides, I'm out of money, so I can't take you anywhere." Contradicting Anthony's belief, Yvette—feeling that she owed him some hospitality—replied, "Na, you can stay if you want. I just felt like that before because I was worried. We don't have to go out; we could hang out here." Since he just got there and at the moment and didn't feel like taking that long train ride back home, Anthony accepted and asked, "Sure, I'll stay. What do you wanna do?" Trying to seem like a responsible parent, Yvette answered, "Well, I gotta take care of my kids. You could watch TV if you want." Having a strong love for children, Anthony—being a guest and trying to be polite—inquired, "Do you need help? To tell you the truth, I'd like to hang out with your kids too. I mean, if that's okay with you."

Having no problem with Anthony taking interest in her kids, Yvette accepted the break and answered, "Sure. Knock yourself out."

Yvette's son, Jose, was only four months old. Since he slept most of the time, the only assistance Anthony could provide was to feed him, change him, and put him to sleep. Gina, on the other hand, was two and needed a lot more attention. After Anthony played a variety of games with her, Gina grew tired. Tucking her into bed, Anthony read her a story until she fell asleep.

Once both kids were asleep, Anthony retired to Yvette's

room. Lying on her stomach on the bed, Anthony sat beside her. Very sincere in his complimenting, Anthony said, "You have great kids. That Gina, she's precious." Rolling her eyes at Anthony's statement, Yvette very crankily replied, "Yeah, right. You try to deal with them every day. Don't get me wrong—I love my kids, but they stress me out so much that I got a permanent pain in my neck and back." Being the polite, good—hearted person he was, Anthony replied to Yvette's statement. "I can help you with that. I give really good massages. Would you like one?" Although she barely knew Anthony, Yvette liked the idea of being pampered, and without hesitating she replied, "Yeah, please. By all means go ahead." Giggling from how Yvette answered, Anthony proceeded to rub her neck and said, "Okay, I took care of your kids and put them to sleep. And now all I have left to do is take care of you, put you to sleep, then my job will be done for tonight, and I'll be on my way."

When done, Anthony rose to his feet and said, "I have to say, Yvette, I had fun playing husband and daddy. Maybe we can do this again sometime." It could have been what he just said, or it could have been that Yvette felt the need to show Anthony some gratitude. It could have been that Yvette truthfully found Anthony attractive, or maybe it was all of these reasons combined that decided the outcome of the rest of the night. Since it was near-impossible to read her, whatever it was that motivated Yvette, it caused her to treat Anthony totally different compared to when he first walked into her apartment. Referring to what Anthony said about playing husband and daddy, Yvette rolled onto her back and responded, "Well, who said you're finished playing? I never said the game was over."

In a situation like this, Anthony would usually think of something witty to say. As Anthony sat frozen for a minute, yet just about to respond to her last statement, Yvette grabbed Anthony by the back of the neck and began kissing him strongly and sensually. Rapidly having his clothes ripped off—much different from anytime he had sex with Juanita—he let Yvette lead and went with it. Once Anthony was naked, Yvette—not being shy at all—removed all of her clothes, and revealed the stupendous body she was blessed with. Still kissing Anthony, Yvette moved her hand down Anthony's body; and when she felt his penis—just as Juanita was surprised the first time by the size—said softly, gasping for air, "Oh my God." Self-conscious and a bit uncomfortable, Anthony replied, "What happened? Is everything alright?" Feeling and caressing Anthony's erection, Yvette answered, "Nothing. It's just you are really big. I never had one this size before." Not sure if it was okay to continue, Anthony inquired, "Do you want me to stop?"

Kissing his neck now and becoming extremely excited while she felt his testicles along with his penis, Yvette whispered in Anthony's ear, "No. Don't stop. Fuck me! Fuck me hard!"

Unlike the all-night romantic lovemaking that Anthony and Juanita had done so often, the sex between Anthony and Yvette ended within the hour. Once penetration began, the two barely kissed each other during the actual act. Remaining in just the one position with him on top, Anthony pumped his manhood deep inside of Yvette. Instructing him to pump it harder and faster, once she reached her climax Yvette pushed Anthony away. Not used to sex being over so fast, and unsatisfied himself, Anthony unsuccessfully attempted to keep going. He even made an effort to switch positions, but Yvette ignored his advances. Leaving Anthony still erect and with a swollen scrotum, Yvette got out of the bed and went to the bathroom.

When she returned wearing a bathrobe, Yvette—yawning and stretching as if she was ready to go to sleep—said, "Aren't you gonna to get dressed?" Usually an easy-going person, Anthony—disappointed by the encounter—displayed it when he asked Yvette, "Oh why? Are we finished?" Offended by Anthony's assumption, Yvette claimed, "If you are expecting to spoon all night, I'm sorry, Anthony, but I don't have guys sleep over. It doesn't look good to my kids." With his defenses up, and feeling the need to set Yvette straight, Anthony responded, "Na, it's not that. I just thought you were taking a break and then would want more." Anthony's comment making her self—conscious about her performance, Yvette inquired, "No way. I'm okay. Didn't you notice how much I came? Why? Wasn't it good enough for you?" In an effort not to lower Yvette's self—esteem, Anthony—his facial expression telling the truth—felt the need to be honest as well. Being accustomed only to how Juanita had been in bed, Anthony—without using his dearly-departed girlfriend's name—explained, "Na it's not that. Yeah, it was good. The only thing is, usually I hold out until the woman cums a few times. So really, I didn't get to finish."

Yvette was astonished by Anthony's claim: This was the first time she had ever beaten a man to an orgasm. Her sexual ability the only weapon she had, Yvette took a lot of pride in it. The anticipation of sex had been the only way Yvette got men to do anything for her. Now Yvette grew worried that she would be unable to use sex to get him to do things for her in the future. Nervous if Anthony left now, she'd never hear from him again, Yvette apologetically claimed, "Oh, I'm so sorry, I didn't know you didn't cum. I feel bad."

Anthony sat on the edge of the bed with a sheet draped over his groin. Yvette moved closer towards him. With her ego at stake, Yvette, dropping to her knees, very sensually explained, "Look, I can't let you fuck me again. Even though I loved it, you are too big and I can't take the pain again right now. But I feel bad about leaving you hard, so you are gonna get off another way."

Slowly lifting the sheet that covered him, Yvette began massaging Anthony's penis and testicles. As she stroked him more firmly, Anthony became completely aroused once again. Once Anthony reached complete erection, Yvette leaned his body back so that he couldn't watch her. While Yvette pleasured Anthony orally, it was obvious to him that she had done this quite often. Even without the luxury of being able to watch her, Anthony felt Yvette using everything to ensure his satisfaction. Unlike with Juanita, there wasn't any need to instruct her on what he enjoyed; it appeared that Yvette already knew. When Anthony told Yvette he was about to ejaculate, she removed her mouth and finished him off by using her hands.

Afterwards, as she wished he would, Anthony greeted then left Yvette for the night. On his way home, Anthony wondered what Yvette's intentions were. At first he found it peculiar that Yvette ever called him at all. Then, once he arrived at her apartment, it was obvious that Yvette needed money from him. What was difficult for Anthony to figure out was why Yvette slept with him after she had already got the money. Could it be that she really did like him? Or did she merely feel obligated? It would all have been easier to understand if Yvette asked for the money after the sex.

Anthony would discover the answer to all these questions later in the relationship. Yvette played the game very well. Using her sexuality, Yvette could get men to do just about anything she wanted them to. But this procedure must have backfired on her some time in the past and, learning from her mistake, Yvette made sure always to get what she wanted before sleeping with a man. Thus she got through life by hooking up with guys who would pay her rent and bills in return for sexual favors. Yvette was an undercover prostitute. The fact that she needed to be somewhat attracted to the guy she was using — she was not willing to sleep with just anybody — separated Yvette from the everyday hooker.

Still, the game had been disrupted from the moment Yvette slept with Anthony. That first night, Yvette noticed that Anthony was generous, caring, considerate, and fun. Watching him with her kids, she knew that Anthony would make a good husband and father. But the coup de grace — the one thing that made all the difference — was that, the moment she slept with him, Yvette fell in love. To most people in general, falling in love is a wonderful experience. Knowing that you have someone special in your life makes everything around much better. Even your worst problems don't seem so bad, since you know you have something to look forward to. Considering the man she was falling in love with was not financially set, falling in love was the exact opposite for Yvette. Having a decent job, and his own place, Anthony had the ability to support Yvette and her children. On the other hand, Anthony would not be able to give Yvette any of the luxuries she felt she deserved. Which brings us to Yvette's major dilemma. Because of her feelings for

Anthony, Yvette's conscience would no longer allow her to live the life she was so accustomed to. No longer was she able to fake her feelings for a man to get him interested, and no longer would Yvette be able to exchange sex with him to get what she wanted.

Since already establishing that she had only used him that night, it was a surprise to Anthony when Yvette called him a couple of weeks later. Suspicious by the phone call, Anthony answered, "Hello." Without wasting any time, Yvette responded, "Hey, its me. Are you busy? Can you come over?" Initially rejecting Yvette's invite to her apartment, Anthony answered, "Na, I'm not busy or nothin. I just don't feel like makin that trip. Why? Is everything okay?" Never being rejected before, and noticing the uncertainty in Anthony's voice, Yvette replied, "Yeah, everything is alright; and no, I don't need any money. But I really got to talk to you, and I can't do it on the phone." After Anthony agreed and arrived at her apartment, Yvette decided to go with the best policy—honesty. Explaining her initial intent with him, and then her present feelings, Yvette assured Anthony, "Look, I admit that at first I only needed you to help me with my phone bill. But my feelings are stronger now. I am not only interested in what you could give me. Do you understand? The thing is, I won't ever be able to see you again unless we are actually together."

"So, that means we are now officially together, right?" Anthony said.

Beginning to undress him, right before the two began consummating the beginning of their relationship, Yvette said, "What did you think?"

It would never be clear to any of Anthony's friends or family members why he chose to be with Yvette. She and Anthony had nothing in common but their physical attraction. And soon Yvette would drop out of school. As all relationships do, Anthony's and Yvette's started off great. With Anthony working nights, and Yvette out of school, and her kids at the babysitter's all day, the two were able to spend the whole day, every day, together—alone and undisturbed. By making the sex better for him, it wasn't long before Yvette was able to gain control over Anthony. Anthony abandoned his roommate to move in with Yvette. Anthony grew attracted to the idea of being a family man.

Unfortunately, and despite all his efforts, once Yvette's initial physical attraction to Anthony faded, so did her happiness. Three years into the relationship, Anthony noticed a dramatic change in Yvette.

Being the greedy, self-centered, egotistic person she was, Yvette never appreciated everything Anthony sacrificed for her. Anthony would return home from work at four in the morning, and then tend to Yvette's baby at eight. Not only did Yvette not feel guilty over Anthony's lack of sleep, she expected it. God forbid if one day he was too tired to wake up and she had to do her own mothering. And although Yvette didn't do anything all day, she expected Anthony to do all the cooking, cleaning, and laundry. So even though Anthony had been determined to make her life as easy as possible, it was funny to him when Yvette complained of boredom. Their most frequent argument arose due to Anthony's inability to take Yvette out on weekends. So after the same routine had persisted for quite some time, Yvette concluded that she was no longer happy. Sure, everything Anthony did for her was good; yes, he was still the best lover she ever had. Yvette, however, wanted all the best material things in life as well.

Through all the physical and verbal abuse, through all the lack of appreciation and respect shown towards him, through all the times Yvette held out sex from him, it would come down to one final incident that would determine Anthony surrendering on keeping the relationship alive. Proving to her that he was a responsible, trustworthy, hardworking young man—because Anthony took care of and loved Yvette's children as if they were his own—when Yvette broke the news to him, it was not only her decision that broke his heart but the way she said it.

"Anthony, I have to tell you something. Look, I was pregnant and I got an abortion. Not because I don't want any more children, because I do. It's because I don't think you're good enough to have a child with."

"Not good enough? After everything I did for you and your family you have the nerve to tell me I am not good enough? I think it is the other way around. It's better that you did get the abortion, because if anything, you're not worthy of carrying my baby." Never believing herself to be wrong, Yvette questioned, "What? You're crazy. So what you took care of me and my kids? That's what a man is supposed to do. It's not my fault you can't make enough money to make me happy." Not allowing the conversation to escalate to where he would do something he'd regret, Anthony simply replied as he walked out the door, "Well, Yvette, no one will ever make enough money to make you happy. People as greedy as you are never satisfied with anything."

Before this, Anthony would have done anything so that he and Yvette could stay together. Even though her treatment towards him had been disrespectful and dishonorable, Anthony—contrary to the opinions of his friends and family—truly believed that there still existed some good in Yvette. Determined to make her happy and prove everyone else to be wrong, Anthony—believing that one day she would snap out of her hostile demeanor—decided he was going to be as patient as he could with Yvette. Like waking up from a hypnotic trance, throwing everything he did out the window in an effort to make this relationship work, Anthony—once he heard the news of the abortion—concluded there wasn't anything he could ever do to make Yvette happy. He no longer believed that he did not deserve better, or that she had any good in her, or—most important—that Juanita would ever have approved of her. It was not so much that Anthony was against abortion. To be denied the opportunity of fatherhood, to be denied consultation in the matter, was the final straw. It was obvious to everyone that Anthony had been an exceptional father-figure to both of Yvette's children. Raising them and supporting them financially, Anthony loved those children as if they were his own. So when Yvette not only decided to get the abortion, but didn't even discuss it with him beforehand, Anthony took it as a slap in the face. Since Yvette had been unable to be honest about it, one could only guess why she would choose not to have Anthony's child. Surely Yvette didn't think that Anthony wouldn't take care of the baby. Was it a question that the baby wouldn't fit into Yvette's busy schedule? Probably not, although her laziness and lack of responsibility certainly factored in on Yvette's decision. Anthony's opinion is the one that made the most sense. Yvette was looking for an escape from the relationship she had with Anthony. Finding another man willing to do everything Anthony did, and who was financially stable, would be Yvette's ultimate goal. Maintaining the only asset she had going for her—her figure—would be the only way Yvette could achieve her goal. Becoming pregnant and having a baby would ultimately ruin any hopes Yvette had of landing another man—hence getting stuck in her current relationship.

When Yvette began to withhold sex, Anthony withheld doing all the chores Yvette had grown accustomed to him doing, including paying for the unnecessary babysitter. Forced to take care of herself, and faced with the stress of dealing with her kids on a daily basis, it wasn't long before Yvette began looking for another man to replace Anthony. But spoiled by Anthony, Yvette had a difficult time finding a suitable replacement. There aren't too many men willing to take care of other men's children, do all the housework, and that allow the mother to sit around the apartment like a princess.

Finally, with no other choice, Yvette turned to her son's father, Jose. After his release from prison, Jose made a good living for himself out in California. Since he was still deeply in love with her, it was easy for Yvette to coerce Jose into promising to do everything Anthony had.

"Look," Yvette told Anthony. "You know it is over between us. I've decided to move to California to marry Jose. I just need one more favor—and I promise, I'll never bother you again. I need you to pay for the plane tickets for me and the kids to get out of here."

After all the arguing, all the downgrading, and all the physical abuse Anthony had to endure, he was more than happy to pay for Yvette and her children to leave. A little confused though, Anthony said, "Sure, I'll pay for them. But I don't understand. You say you're leaving me to be with someone who has more money. Why can't he pay for the tickets?" Attempting to avoid answering, coming off with an attitude, Yvette responded, "Look, if you don't want to pay, just be a man and say so. Jose wouldn't ask why, he'd just do it. That's why I'm gonna be with him and not you. I just don't want to ask him." In an effort to not prolong the inevitable, Anthony replied.

"You know what? Forget about it. I said I'll pay, and I will. To tell you the truth, I don't care about the money. It's none of my business why he can't pay. Let's just get it over with. I'll pick up the tickets before work tomorrow." Realizing that there wouldn't be any happiness in a future with Yvette, Anthony welcomed the end of this four-year relationship. He found it very odd what Yvette chose to do next. Never doing it in the past, maybe Yvette was planning ahead in case that it didn't work out with Jose. Or maybe Yvette knew that the game was over and she could finally treat Anthony like a human being. Whatever it was that possessed her, Yvette—at the airport while saying goodbye to him—actually said, "Thank you, Anthony. I know I never said this before. And I know you think I never appreciated you, but even though it is kinda late now, thank you for everything you did for me over the years." Being too little too late to show her appreciation, Anthony had been too skeptical to be touched by Yvette's display of gratitude. Being polite, yet not meaning it, Anthony replied, "You're welcome, Yvette. For whatever reason you never showed any appreciation, it's okay. If it was a problem, I would have said something. Let's just move on from here with no hard feelings."

Not looking back, Anthony walked away from Yvette and looked forward to the rest of his life without her.

With extra money in his pocket now, Anthony spent a lot of time at the beach. Buying a well-restored Chevy Monte Carlo and cruising around the streets of the neighborhood, Anthony had no trouble meeting women. As word spread of his sexual ability and the equipment that he had been blessed with, women from all around the neighborhood attempted to get to know Anthony. It became frustrating for him. He was looking for the perfect woman, and he turned a lot away.

Spanish descent, brown eyes, dark hair, and dark skin were just a few of the characteristics that Anthony's perfect girl had to possess. She had to be between 5'2" and 5'5", weigh no more than 120 pounds, possess at least a C-size bra cup, have a small waistline and round yet plump and firm buttocks. Once he found a woman matching this description, he would also require her to have a winning personality. That is to say, she could be confident in her beauty but not stuck up. And all of these qualities would mean nothing to Anthony unless she appreciated everything he did for her and was willing to do the same for him. After searching for a few months, Anthony concluded that such a woman no longer existed. And, desperate for love, Anthony once again made one of the biggest mistakes of his life.

Shortly after their reconciliation, Jose in California broke up with Yvette. With nobody else to turn to, Yvette took a chance and tried to convince Anthony to come out there.

Anthony answered his phone one day to a crying Yvette.

"Hello, babe," she said. "I need to talk to you." Noticing the stress in Yvette's voice and having a soft spot in his heart for her, Anthony replied, "What's wrong? Is everything okay? How are the kids?" In an effort to obtain Anthony's pity, Yvette—continuing to cry—explained, "The kids, they're fine; but me, no, I am not. Babe, Jose dumped me. You were right about me. No man will ever want me the way I am. This motherfucker made all these promises to me, then once he got what he wanted from me he started treating me like shit. Look, I am so sorry for how I treated you. I had a good thing with you and I blew it."

Yvette succeeding in her attempt, Anthony—believing her eyes were opened concerning himself—replied, "Look, Yvette, I wouldn't say you blew it. I never said I wouldn't be willing to give it another shot. But if I do, then you are gonna have to do things different." As she normally did, blaming something else for the reason, Yvette proclaimed, "I know, and as long as

I am not in New York, my attitude will be different. It's just that living there makes me so stressed out that I take my anger out on other people. I am doing so much better out here with work, with school, with everything. I know if we are together out here, we won't have any problems." Attracted to the idea of living in beautiful, sunny California, yet skeptical about getting back together with Yvette, Anthony replied, "Look, Yvette, this is a big move for me. I can't answer yes or no right now. Let me think about it, and I'll give you an answer in a few days."

After pleading her case with him, and apologizing a thousand times, Anthony decided to give Yvette a second chance. So he quit his job, packed up his life, and started a new one in California.

"I'm so glad you came," Yvette told him. "This is like a dream come true. You'll see how happy we're gonna be."

"I hope so. I mean, that's why I am here, so both of us could be happy, just like we were when we first started."

Yvette did shower Anthony with love at first. But her phoniness would not last. Allowing Anthony to have the upper hand with her got old really fast. Yvette could never truly be happy unless she were getting spoiled. It was not in her nature to have to please. And once she believed she had Anthony back, Yvette returned to her former ways. She quit her job, dropped out of school, and made sure Anthony once again carried the financial load. To alleviate her boredom, Yvette made certain word got back to Jose that Anthony had returned. Yvette was not concerned whether Anthony or Jose would win; it was a big deal for her to have two men willing to give anything to win her heart. The competition added excitement to an otherwise empty life, and Yvette kept the game going as long as she could. But after losing trust in Yvette, and feeling betrayed, Anthony realized that the trophy he would acquire by winning the game not worth the effort of playing.

But since Yvette needed this type of chaos in her life, Anthony knew she would do anything to prevent him from leaving, including be dishonest and crafty. So without telling her where or when, Anthony left California. Determined to go where Yvette could not find him, Anthony moved to Virginia, where Joseph lived with his family. One morning Anthony called him from the road at 3:00 in the morning. Joseph Jr. answered the phone half-asleep. "Hello. Who the fuck is this?" Realizing now the time difference, Anthony—very apologetic—replied, "I'm sorry, Joey. I didn't remember it's later there." Disturbed, yet happy to hear from his little brother, Joseph changed his tone and replied, "Na, it's alright. I was still up anyway. What's the matter?" With shame in his voice, and quite embarrassed to ask, Anthony inquired, "Joey, I was wondering if it would be okay if I could crash at your house a while. I left Yvette and I don't want her to know where I went. I figured to just start a new life in Virginia, but I am kinda broke, so I was thinking if I could stay with you a bit until I get back on my feet."

Not doing so well himself, and in desperate need of another income, Joseph said, "Yeah, of course you can. Matter of fact, I could get you a job where I work as soon as you get here. When do you think you will make it here?" Assuming that Joseph Jr. had still been in the Navy, a confused Anthony replied, "I should be there in about three days. What do you mean get me a job? Where? In the Navy?" Setting Anthony straight, Joseph Jr. explained, "Na, you didn't know? I got kicked out of the Navy. I'm working for a shelving place now. The pay ain't so good, but there is a lot of overtime. I'll explain everything when you get here."

Anthony arrived in Virginia a few days later, and Joseph explained that he was kicked out of the Navy for smoking marijuana. He was now working for Lately Distributors, a leading shelving company in Virginia Beach. His wife, Nadi, much like Yvette, could not hold a job, leaving the majority of the financial responsibility to Joseph. Once Joseph got Anthony a job, Anthony began helping with the rent and the bills. Living with his brother's family did not leave Anthony too much time to have a social life. The closest Anthony came to having a relationship was when he met one of Nadi's friends, Kelly. Except for her Spanish descent, Kelly possessed every quality, physical and otherwise, of Anthony's perfect woman.

Her sexy southern accent and revealing clothing attracted Anthony to her immediately. The feeling mutual, one night while drinking and playing cards, after everyone else had gone to sleep, Kelly made her move on Anthony. Noticing Anthony tense from his occupation, Kelly inquired, "Do you need a massage?" Accepting the gesture without question, Anthony replied, "Yeah, please."

Kelly sat on the couch and Anthony sat on the floor between her legs. Already loose from the alcohol, Anthony leaned back onto Kelly's vagina. At that point, Kelly moved her hands from Anthony's back down his chest and began kissing him.

After breaking the ice of the first kiss, Anthony turned around and went immediately for Kelly's breast. Once he had her topless as he was, Kelly—without thinking twice—unzipped Anthony pants.

Pulling out Anthony's erect penis and reacting just like all the other woman before her, Kelly gasped and said, "Oh my gosh, I never seen one like this before. Do you have something?" she said—meaning a condom. Not possessing any protection, hoping she might, Anthony explained, "Na, I'm sorry. I wasn't expecting to be with anyone for a while." Although Kelly was disappointed with Anthony's lack of protection, once she felt his size she grew determined to have Anthony inside of her. Gasping for air, she replied, "Well, you're okay, right? Please, though, I can't get pregnant, so don't cum in me. Alright?" Concerned about Kelly now, Anthony inquired, "What about you? Are you alright?" As she took off her panties and got ready to take Anthony in, Kelly proclaimed, "Yeah, I'll explain why later. C'mon, let's do it." Trusting her statement, Anthony mounted Kelly and proceeded to have sex with her.

Afterward, Anthony and Kelly got dressed so nobody would know what they had done. Recalling Kelly's statement, Anthony inquired, "What did you mean when you said it's okay, you'll explain later?" With a guilty expression on her face, hoping Anthony wouldn't bring it up, Kelly replied, "Anthony, I like you a lot. I was just dying to kiss your perfect lips. But once I felt your dick, I couldn't resist. The thing is, I can't have anything serious with you. I know I should have said something before, but I am married." Surprised, but not angry, losing respect for Kelly, Anthony asked, "Really? Where is your husband now, though?" Observing the disappointment in Anthony's face, and feeling bad, Kelly responded, "Oh, I'm so sorry. My husband is in the Navy and has been out on leave for the last six months. I never cheated on him before. And like I said, I was just gonna kiss you, but after feeling your dick, I just got so horny. I mean, I just had to. I mean, I don't care or nothing. My husband cheats on me too; I just should have told you before."

Anthony would have probably not gotten serious with Kelly anyway, and so he wasn't heartbroken. But the fact that he was being used once again caused him to develop a low opinion of himself.

Once fully dressed, Anthony, being polite, replied, "Thank you, Kelly. I'm glad you told me now before I got attached. I did have a good time, and I hope everything works out for you and your husband."

With nothing else to look forward to now in Virginia, and feeling homesick, Anthony headed back to New York. Only away from home a total of nine months, considering everything that happened during those months, Anthony felt as if he had just spent a lifetime away from home.

Upon returning, being the exceptional worker that he was, Anthony was with no hesitation whatsoever accepted back into the company he'd worked at before his excursion around the country. After the initial "welcome back Anthony" celebrations were over, life for Anthony had once again become repetitious and boring as it was before he left. But still unable to find that perfect somebody, Anthony discontinued his efforts altogether. Concentrating on his work, Anthony began to put aside money towards his future. Now that all his friends were getting older, and the relationships they had been in were getting serious, Anthony found himself alone more often than not.

About a year later, Anthony began to evaluate his life. Having spent so much of his time at work, Anthony established himself as one of the company's top assets. But Anthony's desire for money was not as strong as his desire for love. Noticing his youth rapidly coming to an end, Anthony began to worry whether or not he'd ever have a family of his own.

Then—just as funny as his life always was—Anthony once again would face the challenge of yet another choice that would alter his life one way or another. At the same time Anthony was offered a management position in his company, Yvette made another attempt to get back into his life. Selling Anthony the same story as she had the last time, Yvette added a twist in her efforts. Surprised by the phone call, Anthony answered the phone regretfully, "Hello." Coming off angry at first—also surprised Anthony answered—Yvette responded, "Hey, it's about time you answered the phone. Were you afraid to talk to me—like you were afraid to face me before you left?" After a year of hiding from Yvette, and believing it was time to face her, Anthony replied, "Matter of fact, yeah."

Surprised, Yvette asked, "Why? Am I evil or something? You can't even talk to me?" Avoiding offending Yvette, yet needing to tell the truth, Anthony answered, "Well, I wouldn't say evil. For me, though, you really aren't healthy. Every time I get involved with you, it becomes a waste of time, and I usually end up regretting it." Never hearing Anthony speak so to the point before, Yvette knew she had to do something else to get Anthony back this time. With sincerity in her voice, Yvette—crying as she spoke—replied, "I'm so sorry, babe. I fucked up so much. My life is over. I threw everything good I had away just to play these childish games. Every day I wish I never got that abortion. If I had your baby, at least you would always be in my life. I prayed to God for forgiveness and promised that if he let me have you back I would make it up to you. I am truly ready to have the family you always wanted." Wanting to believe Yvette so much, before just hanging up on her, Anthony asked, "Are you serious? So you're saying if I get back with you, you'll have my baby?" Knowing this was her only chance, Yvette replied without thinking twice. "Yeah. I want to have another child right now. But I know I won't ever find a better father than you. So the ball is in your court. I am giving you the opportunity if you want it." Skeptical because he couldn't ever believe Yvette again, Anthony replied, "Look, Yvette. I am kinda busy right now. Let me call you later and we'll talk about it more." Agreeing, Yvette and Anthony both hung up their phones respectfully, only to have this conversation become ongoing.

Knowing that having someone to bare his child was Anthony's biggest dream, and having no other tricks up her sleeve, each time they spoke on the phone for the next few weeks, Yvette played that card to the bone. Putting Anthony in a position to make yet another major choice in his life, Yvette would not give up. So that he would still be able to keep his job as well, the best thing for Anthony would be if Yvette relocated back to New York. Insuring that Jose was out of the picture would be another plus for Anthony if Yvette were to come back to New York. Basing her reason to want to stay in California strictly on the opportunities available to her, Yvette insisted that Jose was no longer a factor. Using the "willing to bare his child" as leverage, Yvette eventually just gave Anthony an ultimatum.

If Anthony had been a smart man, he'd realize that accepting Yvette's ultimatum would be a huge gamble. If she truly wanted to be with him, Yvette would go anywhere to do so. If Anthony had been a suspicious man, he would haved guessed that—because of the fact that not only his business was set up out there in California, his whole family was out there as well—Jose could never truly be out of the picture. If Anthony had been a cold-hearted man, the moment Yvette called crying, he would have hung-up the phone on her and let her realize what she had in him was now gone. The fact of the matter is, Anthony wasn't any of these men. Indeed sad—but very much true—at the moment Anthony was a very desperate man—desperate because he had not found the woman he was looking for, and desperate because he had seen all his friends plan their weddings and have kids, and desperate because he had missed out on the love that only a woman could give to a man. Convincing himself that he was still young enough to start a new career, yet too old to start a new relationship, Anthony's heart would overcome his need to succeed. So after two weeks of Yvette's phone calls, and despite the advice of his friends, family and co-workers, once again Anthony set out for California.

Believed by many to be a fool, Anthony had no choice but to agree with them. Kicking himself in the head shortly after his arrival to California, Anthony found himself in the same situation he had run away from the previous time.

Arriving home from work one day, Anthony found it odd when he opened up the front door to enter the house and heard the back door slam. Reacting other than Yvette may have wanted him to, Anthony just calmly asked, "Was somebody just here?" As she always did when asked a question she didn't want to answer, Yvette angrily responded, "No, Anthony, no one was here. You gonna start this shit already? If you don't trust me, why did you bother to come out here?" After years of knowing Yvette's pattern—feeling in his heart she was lying and yet about to let it go—Anthony replied, "What? What is the problem? It is just a simple question. I ain't accusing you of nothin."

Just when Yvette was about to retaliate with what she believed would be the last word, her son came running into the room to greet Anthony. Since he didn't talk much the last time she had been involved with Anthony, Yvette wasn't counting on her son talking now. Without being asked, Yvette's very excited son announced, "I saw my daddy today."

To avoid, the little boy from getting too much involved, Anthony just asked simply, "Really? What did yous two do? Did you have fun?" Seeming harmless before he asked—and only doing so to change the subject—if Anthony had known ahead of time how Yvette's son was going to answer, and what was going to happen when he did, Anthony would have chosen something different to talk about. In no way trying to tell on his mother, and not knowing there was anything wrong with it, Yvette's son answered Anthony's question. "No, I didn't have no fun. Daddy and Mommy just went to sleep in her room."

Having just been been unwittingly ratted out by her own son, Yvette slapped him across the face.

"You stupid little bastard!" she cried. "You had to say something? You couldn't just keep your mouth shut?"

Yvette tried to strike him again, but before she could do so Anthony grabbed her by the arm. Disturbed by what he had just witnessed, Anthony—just about to lose his mind—screamed,

"What the fuck is wrong with you? You're pissed at him? He didn't know. If there is anyone you should be mad at, it's yourself. I swear, if you lay one more hand on him I'll kill you."

Yvette broke free from Anthony's grasp and stormed into her room.

After tending to the frightened little boy, Anthony collected his thoughts and tried to figure out what to do next. After thinking about it a little while, Anthony—to cover his own end and to ensure the kids were out of harm's way—called the police for the first time ever in his life. Explaining the whole story to they arrived, Yvette was a totally different person.

"Look, I'm sorry," Yvette told them with an air of calmness. "I overreacted. I was angry, and I lost my head for a minute. You can ask anyone. I never did nothing like this before, and won't ever again." Being an out-of-the-ordinary situation, the police were confused what they should do. In an effort to settle this without too much drama, the police turned to Anthony and asked, "Well, you know her the best. What do you think? If we left, do you believe the kids will be okay? Look, we're not looking to lock anybody up. Our only concern is for the kids. So answer honestly, otherwise it will be on your head."

"Yeah," Anthony said. "Honestly, yeah. I'll tell you why too. She's angry because of me. Look, the only thing I want to do is leave. Once I'm gone, out of her life, she'll stay calm and the kids will be fine." Accepting Anthony's answer, the police turned back towards Yvette for her to agree, and asked, "Is this true? So he's leaving, and you're going to be okay? Right?"

As Yvette nodded her head to the police a tear rolled down her cheek. Since she hadn't kept her end of the bargain, Yvette—realizing she had nothing left to convince him into giving her any more chances—could only watch the police escort Anthony out of her life forever. Even though that would be the last straw for

Yvette, there would be no way Anthony could return home to New York and face all the "I told you so" speeches awaiting him. With little alternative, Anthony decided to return to Virginia and live the remainder of his life there.

Unfortunately, many things had changed since he was last there. For starters, although Anthony's Monte Carlo had been reliable in the past, it was unable to make that last trip across country. It broke down somewhere in Nebraska, and Anthony was forced to abandon the car and make the rest of the trip by Greyhound. Without a vehicle of his own, Anthony had to rely on Joseph for transportation in Virginia. As for Joseph, unable any longer to afford the house he was renting, he had moved his family to a less expensive trailer park. Anthony quickly learned that all the stereotypes about trailer parks were true. After living with his brother for the next two years, Anthony learned that Joseph Jr. had become their father. He answered perfectly that tired cliché "Like father like son"; though considering the hate Joseph had for their father, one would have thought he'd have treated his family better.

Spending all his money on alcohol, strip clubs, and whatever drug was available, Joseph Jr. stole anything he thought he could sell in order to support his habits. Using their father as his excuse, Joseph Jr. proclaimed he was beyond help. Selling it only to himself, Joseph Jr. believed that his addictions were genetic. Anthony soon realized his brother was not going to change. Constantly being called upon to assist Joseph Jr. in taking care of his family, by living with him Anthony's life would never amount to anything. Always willing to help out anyone, anytime, Anthony was very easy to take advantage of. That being the case, as long as he had Anthony there to help him out financially, Joseph continued to live his life the way he wanted to. Once Anthony discovered his money had begun to disappear, he realized it was time to move on. Regardless of the numerous pleas by Joseph Jr. to get him to stay in Virginia, Anthony—in a no-win situation—made up his mind to move back to New York.

Reluctant to work for the same company he'd worked for

so many years prior, Anthony sought employment elsewhere. But since the job market was so tight and he was desperate for money, Anthony had no choice but to go back to work there. Just as before, the company had been more than happy to put Anthony back on the payroll. Realizing his worth, the company—in an effort to keep him from leaving again—did not waste any time in giving Anthony a management position. It wasn't too often that Anthony was right about any choice he made. After everything was said and done, Anthony was able to go right back where he was before he left, hence proving that there wasn't any harm done careerwise by Anthony turning down the position to go chase love across the country. Only costing him time and money, Anthony would never have to live with regret that he didn't at least try.

Although he still dated, as the years went by Anthony had totally given up on love. Believing his one and only opportunity for true love had passed with Juanita, Anthony's expectations of women were extremely low. He kept a small phonebook loaded with women's numbers and limited his involvement with them to casual sex. In most cases, all the women with whom he had relations accepted Anthony's sole interest with complete understanding and enthusiasm. It is surprising how many women were not looking for a relationship and were interested in just having good sex. At work, Anthony continued to receive promotions. Promoted and awarded so many times, going as far as he'd be able to go in the company, life at work became boring for Anthony. With the constant repetition of his job function, there were no more challenges left for him.

It is always amazing how life works out sometimes—how you find something when you are not looking for it; and when you're looking for it, you can't find it anywhere. Then there is fear—the things in life you should fear, you don't; and the things you don't fear, you should. Then there is the biggest one—sometimes you want something so much, you'll do anything for it; then once you get it, you find that you really didn't want it at all; then you would do anything to get rid of it. Certainly everyone encountered the following one time or another in their lives. Anthony, on the other hand, would wind up experiencing them all at once.

Anthony worked very hard to get where he was in the company. After numerous pleas, and resigning twice in order to chase love and explore other options, Anthony was finally given the position he so very much deserved. However, because of all the stress that came along with the job, Anthony had become miserable. There were times when, unable to sleep, Anthony lay awake all day in bed, wishing he'd remained just a regular worker. With love now a distant memory, and having everything he wanted, Anthony no longer had anything to look forward to. Going crazy in his life, and slacking off at work, Anthony seriously contemplated making a career move or relocating his residence. Having that empty feeling from not being the husband and father he so much longed to be, Anthony—in order to fill that empty void—even considered getting back together with Yvette.

And just at that moment when he believed he could no longer take it, into his life walked Patricia, the most beautiful girl alive. Of Columbian descent, she resembled Juanita in every way. Her first day working for the company as a driver, Anthony introduced himself to her right away. Unfortunately, the initial conversation could not go any further than the introduction. Only able to find out her name was Patricia, this perfect-looking woman only had one flaw: she spoke little to no English at all. Observing that the physical attraction was indeed mutual, and although his ability to speak Spanish had been limited, Anthony was still determined to develop a relationship with Patricia.

Knowing he would not be able to speak verbally to Patricia, Anthony realized the only means of communication with her would be through writing. At first Anthony attempted to enlist one of his Spanish friends to translate his letters. Unfortunately this friend translated only the words he thought Patricia might like and did not translate the letter correctly. When Anthony wrote, "I'd like to get to know you better," Anthony's friend translated it to "I want to love you forever." So, not wanting to give Patricia the wrong idea, Anthony looked for another means of translating his words. Finally—through another friend—Anthony discovered a website that could translate anything he wanted to say from English to Spanish and back again. Working out perfectly, the use of this web site led Anthony and Patricia to write each other every day. Each letter becoming heavier than the last, Anthony and Patricia were able to find out everything there was to know about each other. Growing very fond of each other, Anthony and Patricia spent every day together doing her route. Within a few months, Patricia would be able to understand English as perfectly as Anthony would understand Spanish.

Although Anthony and Patricia very much wanted to be together, their relationship was stalled from the outset due to Patricia being in the middle of a divorce—their relationship never got passed the friendship stage. Patricia's problems soon became more severe. Living with a man she no longer loved, Patricia was made to feel extremely uncomfortable by him and his family. In an effort to keep her daughter away from the tension, Patricia sent her to live with her mother in Colombia. Unable to think about love and unsure how long she would continue to reside in the United States, Patricia rejected all Anthony had to offer and broke it off with him. Remaining friends, Anthony supported Patricia and continued to assist her with anything she needed.

Once again Anthony's heart had been broken. Although never developing the relationship he wanted to with her, Anthony truly did love her. Because of everything he did for her, Patricia—still having some feelings for him—really did not want to hurt Anthony. Knowing her dilemma and accepting her decision, Anthony, although hurt, did not hold anything against her. Because he'd been hurt a lot worse in the past than from the recent pain inflicted at the hands of Patricia, I wouldn't consider that the break up with her was what made Anthony flip. However, the break-up would be significant. It marked the beginning of the string of bad luck that would soon plague Anthony's life. Without Patricia by his side, Anthony would not be able to withstand the life-altering events which followed soon after.

Shortly after Patricia's decision, Anthony would suffer yet another loss. Still continuing to help Patricia with her route, Anthony had been sacrificing a lot of sleep to do so. Not to say that he would have heard the alarm go off on his Ford Explorer if he hadn't been so tired, but maybe the neighborhood kids wouldn't have stole it if they hadn't known Anthony's daily routine. Taking for granted that he lived in a decent neighborhood, Anthony didn't think much of it when he wa watched parking his car that morning by the neighborhood kids. Arriving home the morning of the incident—factoring in the hours he helped Patricia with her route—Anthony had just completed a sixteen-hour workday. With the same amount of work awaiting him the next day, Anthony only had sleep on his mind. Considering that Anthony arrived home and was asleep by four in the morning, and that the rest of his block was awake by five, although it could be determined the time his car was stolen and by whom, it could not, however, be proven. The only logical explanation was that the car was stolen by the kids hanging out when Anthony had arrived home.

People who drive never realize how important their vehicle is until they no longer have it. In most cases, owning a vehicle is more a luxury than it is a necessity. Sure, it is more convenient having a car; however, with public transportation the way it is, people can still get around without one. However, life without a car would be more difficult for Anthony. Living in New York and working nights in New Jersey, although he had access to public transportation, it was limited. Having to take a bus and three trains each way, the total traveling time for Anthony exceeded five hours total. With no other choice, Anthony planned to travel to and from work until he could either get a new car or a new job.

Fortunately—and at the same time unfortunately—by adding on yet another loss, Anthony's problem solved itself. No longer would he have to spend all those hours traveling to and from work. No longer would he have to worry—for no reason whatsoever—about his train breaking down in a tunnel. And best of all, no longer would Anthony need to worry about all the loss of sleep which stemmed from the extra hours put in at work. All theses issues, and then some, were solved when for no reason at all—after all the years of hard work, dedication and loyalty—the Anthony was laid off the day he returned from his rarely-taken vacation. The only reason his boss gave him was that Anthony disobeyed some company policy. It wasn't that Anthony was worried about losing the job that he didn't like anyway. What hurt him the most, after all the back breaking work and sacrifices he made for them over the years, was being fired for an insufficient reason.

After leaving the company and collecting unemployment, Anthony once again had to reassess his life. Attempting to live a good life, and doing everything the right way, was not working out for Anthony at all. Throughout his life, despite being good to everyone, Anthony had been mistreated continuously—by teachers, by family members, by women, and now by employers. At what point does a person snap? How much misfortune and heartache can one endure before inadvertently losing his mind? After hearing his story, my guess was that Anthony's last straw would come after losing his girlfriend, his car, and his job all in the same month. Standing corrected, it turned out Anthony was a lot tougher than I had thought. Not true in all cases—but after listening to the incident that determined the fate that Anthony faces today, I could only come to one conclusion. Anyone can endure anything when he truly has nothing to lose. Through all the pain—physical and emotional—that Anthony suffered throughout his life, through all the bad experiences he'd encountered, and all the incorrect decisions he'd mistakenly made, none would ever be as severe as the last one.

While he sat at home one Saturday watching the Red Sox tie the Yankees in a game right before the All Star break, Anthony's phone rang. It was Josephina. Very rarely doing so, Anthony—for a reason that to this day is still unknown—picked up the ringing phone in his house. Hearing the disturbed voice of Josephina crying on the other end, Anthony inquired,

"Hello, Josephina. Is that you?" Unable to hold back her tears, and finally finding the courage, Josephina said, "Anthony, I have terrible news. Mommy's dead."

Dropping to the ground in disbelief, making sure he'd heard correctly, Anthony responded, "What? Say that again. Please let this be a mistake." Unfortunately, though, it wasn't. Becoming a little less hysterical, Josephina replied, "No, Anthony. I'm so sorry, it isn't. She's gone, she's really gone." In an effort not to offend his mistake-prone sister, needing to find out everything for himself, Anthony demanded, "Look, where are yous? I'm coming there right away." After retrieving the address to the hospital from his sister, Anthony rushed there as fast as he could. Unfortunately, this time—to Anthony's distress—Josephina had not made any mistakes.

Once Anthony arrived to the hospital, the rest of his family came rumbling in as well.

Loved by everyone, Angela caused a lot of sadness when she passed. Probably where Anthony developed the trait, Angela—to the point where she even took the responsibility in raising her late sister's children—had always been willing to help everyone she could. Much too young to die, the worst thing about it was that Angela died unexpectedly. To this day it is not understood why Angela never disclosed her condition to her family. Was smoking that important to her? Was she more comfortable having the cancer rip her lungs apart than being forced to quit smoking by those who loved her? Or did she believe that, after smoking for fifty years, it would be almost impossible to quit? Maybe keeping her secret had nothing to do with wanting to quit smoking at all. Knowing his mother's pride, it was just that Angela hated to be pitied. On her own since her husband left, Angela would not allow Anthony—or anyone else, for that matter—to pamper her. Although it may sound selfish—and maybe it would have been easier for everyone else to handle her death if they had known in advance that she was going to die—Angela would not have been able to live her life in the manner she had been accustomed to. I mean, really, how much easier would it have been to accept her death if the family had known of her condition? There will still be sadness and all the crying that comes along with it. The only difference would be the length of time in which these feelings were felt. If Angela had told everyone of her condition, not only would they not allow her to continue living the remainder of her life the way she wanted, no one would ever show her their happiness the remaining days of her life.

All said and done, the funeral was a very beautiful one. Sixty-five years worth of friends and family crowded the church and parlor as well. But out of all the people at Angela's funeral, the one who was affected the most was Joseph Jr. Moving his family back to New York while his mother was still alive, Joseph Jr. for the first time ever had finally been able to get his life on track and make Angela proud. He no longer followed the pattern of their father and became the responsible male role model for his kids that he and his siblings never had. One could only imagine the guilt Joseph Jr. must have felt. For many years, because of his way of life, Joseph Jr. caused Angela a lot of worry and stress. Whether or not he played a part in Angela smoking more, surely his lifestyle didn't help any.

Unfortunately just as everything else in Anthony's life, his own mother's funeral would be ruined as well. Adding to everything he lost in his life—none of which was unbearable by itself—but when combined together it would detonate the ticking time bomb which had existed inside of Anthony for some time now. And what could have lit the fuse better than the man who hadn't shown his face in thirty years deciding to walk into the room as if he had never done anything wrong? Only being recognized and greeted by Catholina, Joseph Sr., showing up drunk, announced, "At least one of my children still have respect." Finding it in bad taste that his father was even there at all, Anthony replied, "Who the fuck you think you are? What are you doing here anyway? Nobody wants you here, and we're definitely not giving you no respect." For some reason, living in the delusional world he did, Joseph Sr. did not feel his kids had the right to talk back to him. Reacting as a father who actually raised his children would, Joseph Sr. replied, "Why do you talk to your father this way? Don't you have any respect for the man who gave you life? I know I raised you better than that." Finding his father's remarks funny, yet at the same time continuing to become angrier, Anthony—pointing to Angela's coffin and referring to her, laughing sarcastically—responded, "My father? Na, you ain't my father. You ain't nothin, and you certainly didn't raise me. She did. So what you gave me life? That don't mean shit. She was my mother and my father." Rowdy from the alcohol, unaware of what he heard and was saying, a very offended Joseph Sr. replied, "I don't have to go nowhere. I was invited by my daughter. You should go. I could see she didn't do such a good job raising you. Some father. I think—"

But before he could finish, Anthony quickly approached him. Fueled by the buried anger of thirty years, he struck Joseph Sr., knocking him to the floor. While being held back by some of the other family members in attendance, Anthony screamed at Joseph Sr.—who had been struggling to come to—loud enough for everyone to hear, and threatened, "Don't you ever talk bad about her again! Matter of fact, if I ever hear anything come out of your mouth about her at all, I'll kill you!"

As for what happened next, only three people would know for sure, and only two of them are still living. When told about Anthony's last conversation as a free man, it made me wonder if he had actually been the true culprit. When answering my final question, Anthony left me even more uncertain. Each of Joseph Sr.'s sons blamed their father for the way their lives turned out. Joseph Jr. blamed his father for his addictions, and Anthony felt himself unprotected in a brutal world that takes advantage of softhearted boys. Was it both of them together? Or, since one of them really didn't have anything going for himself while the other did, would one take the blame himself? It wouldn't be the first time.

Escorted to the bathroom to wash his hands, Anthony asked his brother, "What did you think? You think I was wrong for hitting him?" Delighted by the search for approval by his little brother, Joseph Jr. answered, "Hell, no. I wish—actually, I mean I should have done it, not you. Maybe not in front of every one like that, but yeah. I don't know what I was thinking just standing there."

No one understood why Joseph Sr. didn't just leave after being punched out, or why he would choose to follow his sons into the bathroom. Was it because of his pride? Did he really think Anthony owed him an apology? Or maybe it was guilt and the knock to head opened his eyes. Maybe Joseph Sr. went into the bathroom to apologize for all the years of abandonment, abuse, and drunkenness—for being a father who totally neglected his responsibility and in a sense, left his wife and his children for dead. Or maybe it wasn't any of the reasons above. Maybe Joseph Sr. just went to the bathroom merely to clean himself up and was unaware of his sons' presence. Whatever it was that possessed Joseph Sr. to walk into that bathroom, the one thing certain is he would not walk back out.

Moments later, the bathroom attendant entered the bathroom to find Anthony and Joseph Jr. standing over their bloody father, who lie dead on the floor. Stunned, the attendant rushed to the phone to call the police. Too ashamed to face everybody attending the funeral, Anthony and Joseph Jr. remained in the original position in which the bathroom attendant discovered them. Before asking any questions, the police made both Anthony and his brother aware of their rights. Even though Joseph Jr. refused to answer when the police asked "What happened here?" they—as did I—would just assume that Anthony had murdered his father.

Before allowing what a jury would assume, Anthony's lawyer would enter a plea of guilty due to temporary insanity. However, because everyone had witnessed the premeditated threat, and the psychiatrist had found Anthony to be of sound mind and body, the judge overruled Anthony's claim and the case went to trial. If he had had any other lawyer, Anthony would probably not have done any time at all. But since he did not have any money and settled for a court-appointed attorney, his chances for winning the case were equivalent to winning the lottery. Though he began by choosing a jury that had been unsympathetic to what Joseph Sr. did to Anthony and his siblings, the lawyer failed to bring up any past experience of neglect. Preoccupied with the temporary insanity plea, the lawyer only focused on what happened the day of the murder. As a result, the jury would decide that Joseph Sr. had not done anything to justify his being killed.

As Anthony's story came to an end, it became my conclusion: Anthony had been in jail for murdering his father. Not for money or laziness, as I at first had believed—Anthony Pagano murdered his father because his father abandoned them and then implied Angela didn't do a good job in raising them. But is it fair to blame Joseph Sr. for changing Anthony's and Joseph Jr.'s lives by abandoning them?

When I thought about everything Anthony did and didn't do after his abandonment, I have concluded that if Joseph Sr. had stayed in the picture, Anthony would never have been hit by a car, would never have been raped, would never have gotten addicted to drugs. Anthony would probably have played in the major leagues, married, had children, and never have known Juanita, Yvette, or Patricia. Then—who knows?—maybe Anthony would have lived a successful and happy life. Or maybe he wouldn't. But one thing is for certain: Anthony would not be in jail right now.

These, of course, are just my opinions.

When I asked Anthony himself, "Do you think your life would have been different if your father had never left?" Anthony—with regret in his eyes—replied, "Well, assuming he wasn't a useless drunk, of course my life would have been different." In an effort to see if Anthony's views were the same as mine, looking for an elaboration, I asked, "Well, then, how so?"

Unlike myself, Anthony did not go into detail. "Putting it simply," he said, "if my father wasn't a drunk and had stayed in the picture, I would have had more opportunities available to me."

Then, trying to find out the answer to the ultimate question—the question that brought me there that day, the whole reason for writing this story—and feeling a mutual comfort with Anthony, I said very bluntly, "I have a good clue why you did, but why would you say you killed your father?" Leaving my mind wondering what really happened in that bathroom, Anthony—to let me know he wasn't lying—looked me dead in the eye and said, "I never said I killed him." After hearing that answer, and attempting to find out more of the truth, I then asked, "But you pleaded guilty to it. Why?"

Becoming very informative and shutting me up for good, Anthony replied, "Pleading guilty doesn't mean I did it. I never told the cops I did it, I never told my lawyer I did it, I never told the judge and jury I did it, and I am not telling you I did it. And I know what you're thinking. If I didn't kill him, then why am I in here? Think about it good. You know the answer. You know my story. Just take a good look at my life—where do other people like me usually end up? On paper, I am just a statistic. It was ridiculous to ever think I had another choice. Yeah, we pretend we do, but in reality we don't. We are what God wants us to be, and our choices are tattooed to us. But since you took the time to find out the truth, I'll just leave it by saying, I never said I did it."